DB4 G.T. Continuation

History in the making

Porter Press International

DB4 G.T. Continuation

History in the making

James Page

Porter Press International

First published in March 2019

978-1-907085-71-0

Published by
Porter Press International Ltd

Hilltop Farm, Knighton-on-Teme, Tenbury Wells, WR15 8LY, UK
Tel: +44 (0)1584 781588   Fax: +44 (0)1584 781630
sales@porterpress.co.uk
www.porterpress.co.uk

Edited by James Page
Design & Layout by Andrew Garman

Printed by Gomer Press Ltd

Contents

Introduction

This is a story that's not just about the Aston Martin DB4 G.T. continuation cars. It's also about the marque's continuing presence in Newport Pagnell and the people who work at the famous old premises on Tickford Street. Aston Martin may now build its new cars at Gaydon – 40 miles or so to the west – but to many enthusiasts the marque will forever be associated with the Buckinghamshire town that boasts a long and proud coachbuilding history – one that stretches back beyond the dawn of motoring.

Aston Martin's move north from Feltham in Middlesex was instigated by David Brown, another key player in this story and the man who drove the company to great heights during the 1950s and '60s. Under Brown's ownership, the company achieved considerable sporting success and made some of its most enduring and sought-after road cars.

The DB4 G.T. straddled both of those worlds. This competition-spec, short-wheelbase version of the standard DB4 was raced by the likes of Stirling Moss and Jim Clark, and was among the last of a dying breed – a car that could comfortably be driven to the track, raced, then driven home again.

Restarting production of such an iconic model was not a decision to be taken lightly. 'Authentic' is a word that you'll hear a lot when you talk to the people who were involved. It had to be done right, from the bodywork to the engine, from the basic structure to the smallest item of trim. Surveying the continuation prototype, one of the engineers remarked that there was nothing on it about which he'd be embarrassed to talk to his 1959 counterpart, that they've not gone away from how a DB4 G.T. should be built. If something's been done differently to how it was in 1959, there's a very good reason for that.

Such has been this pursuit of authenticity that any description of the period DB4 G.T. cannot be separated from the continuation car, so that is how they will be presented here – side by side. And neither can you appreciate the model's significance without placing it in the wider context of Aston Martin's long history. The importance of honouring that history was something that added extra pressure to everyone involved.

James Page
January 2019

Part 1
SETTING THE SCENE

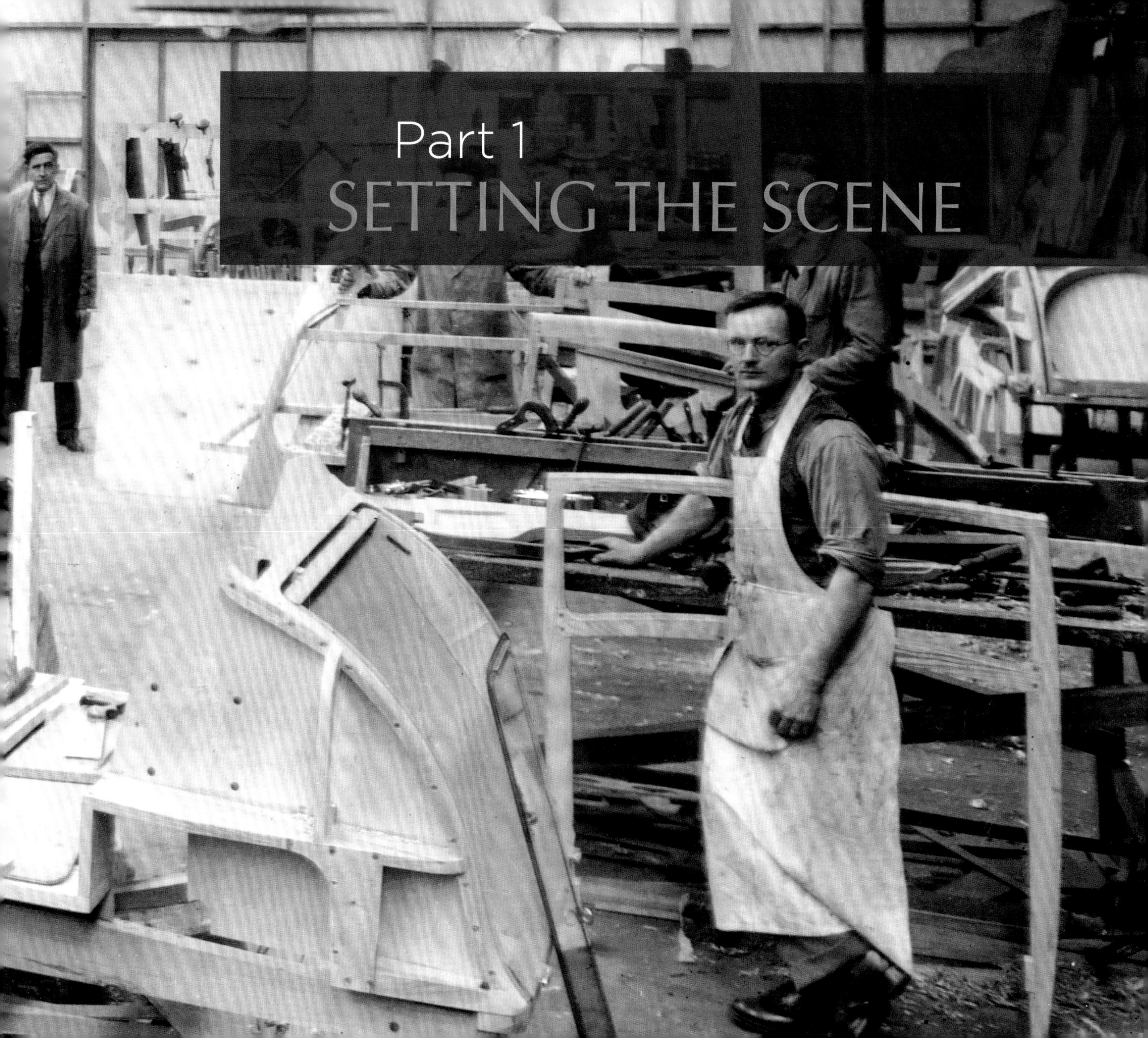

Chapter 1
A HISTORY OF SUCCESS

The DB4 G.T. is one of the greatest cars to be produced by a marque that has motorsport in its DNA. From its very earliest days, and through a variety of owners during subsequent decades, competition has been at the core of what Aston Martin does. Even its name was inspired by a hillclimb venue that quite possibly would otherwise have been long forgotten.

Born on 15 March 1878, Lionel Martin had what could be termed a comfortable upbringing. His father, Edward, owned Martin Brothers – a china clay merchant that was based at St Austell in Cornwall – as well as the Lee Moor brickworks near Plymouth. His mother Elizabeth came from Manchester, and her family was similarly affluent. Her father, William Singleton Birch, had been a successful mineral merchant.

William was also the founder of Singleton Birch Ltd, which quarried lime and chalk in Lincolnshire. When he died in 1881, control of the company passed to his eldest son William Arthur then, when *he* died just two years later, to the youngest son – Thomas Henry. The intention, in time, was for Thomas Henry to pass his majority shareholding to the founder's grandson, who was then just a small boy – Lionel Walker Birch Martin.

Lionel grew up in London and was educated at Eton before studying at Brasenose College, Oxford. As a young man, he became an enthusiastic cyclist and later joined the Bath Road Club, a west London cycling group that had been founded in 1886 and which can also count among its alumni the Marquess of Queensbury – of boxing fame – and William Hinds, founder of the Hammer film company.

It was through the Bath Road Club that Martin met Montague Napier and went into business selling his eponymous cars. More significantly, Martin also met fellow member, and engineer, Robert Bamford. In 1913, the two friends became partners in a garage that was based in Kensington's Henniker Mews and sold Calthorpe, GWK and Singer cars. Although most of Martin's early competition outings had been on two wheels, in 1912 he'd bought a 10hp Singer at the Motor Show and had it tuned by works foreman Jack Addis.

On 4 April 1914, Martin took the Singer to Aston Hill. The venue, near Aston Clinton in Buckinghamshire, was one of dozens of hillclimbs that were scattered around the UK until the use of mainland public roads for such events was banned in 1925. He returned on 16 May for the Herts County Automobile & Aero Club meeting, and his success at the hill would be immortalised in the name of Bamford and Martin's own cars, plans for which were well under way.

Their intention was to fit a 1,389cc, four-cylinder, sidevalve engine that had been specially produced by Coventry Simplex into a chassis of their design. Before the latter was ready,

It was Lionel Martin's success at Aston Hill that gave the marque its name, and his drive that made its cars a production reality in the 1920s. *AMHT*

however, they took the new powerplant and put it into an ageing Isotta Fraschini chassis, Martin driving the hybrid prototype to Brighton in October 1914. By March 1915, the Bamford and Martin chassis was complete, the Simplex engine was fitted, and the first Aston Martin – registered AM4656 and named to celebrate those earlier hillclimb outings – was born. Its appearance earned it the nickname 'Coal Scuttle'.

Due to the Great War, it would be 1920 before Bamford and Martin completed their second prototype, but Bamford left the company – which had relocated to Abingdon Road in Kensington – the following year. His place as a director was taken by Katherine, Lionel's second wife. His first, Christine, had died in 1914, shortly after giving birth to their son John.

Martin continued to use motorsport as a testing ground for his early prototypes. These included 'Bunny' – a short-chassis car that set numerous records at Brooklands – and 'A3', which is now the oldest known survivor.

Then there was the racing car that was commissioned by Count Louis Zborowski so that the immensely wealthy young man could compete in the 1922 French Grand Prix. Zborowski, who in 1911 inherited a vast fortune as well as a chunk of Manhattan, had also built aero-engined leviathans such as 'Chitty Bang Bang' and the Higham Special. He'd even go on to race at Indianapolis, but his early support of Aston Martin was vital for the young firm.

Frustratingly, the two twin-overhead-camshaft cars that were built for the French race – one for Zborowski, one for Clive Gallop – both retired with engine problems. Zborowski would go on to enter the Aston Martin in the Penya Rhin Grand Prix – where he finished second – and the Shelsley Walsh hillclimb.

Actual production didn't get under way until 1923, and only about 53 road cars were completed over the next couple of years. Customers had the option of a 38bhp long-chassis car or a sportier 45bhp short-chassis version, but Martin was struggling to stay afloat. The Honourable John Benson had joined the board thanks to an injection of finance from his mother, Lady Charnwood, and also became chief engineer.

In 1925, Aston Martin made its first appearance at the Motor Show, but shortly afterwards – on 11 November – it went into receivership. The relationship between Martin and Benson unravelled spectacularly. Martin left the company that he'd founded and, in 1926, successfully sued Benson for slander after a number of ill-advised remarks.

It was a sad end to Lionel's involvement in Aston Martin,

but he threw himself into running Singleton Birch Ltd, becoming the majority shareholder in 1929. He also remained a keen motorsport enthusiast, joining the RAC Competitions Committee and becoming a member of the British Racing Drivers Club. During the 1930s, he and Katherine competed in the Alpine Trial and even the Monte Carlo Rally, before the outbreak of World War Two led to him returning to his first love of cycling. He even rejoined the Bath Road Club.

On 14 October 1945, Martin was knocked off his trike near his home in Kingston-upon-Thames and died from his injuries a week later. He was 67.

Lord Charnwood, meanwhile, had bought Aston Martin's assets, but the receiver then put the company up for sale. Vauxhall expressed an interest, as did the Bristol Aeroplane Company – some 20 years before that firm would establish its own car division.

In the end, however, Aston Martin would be saved by two private individuals who'd only recently gone into business together. William Somerville Renwick had worked at Armstrong-Siddeley, which is where he met Augustus Cesare Bertelli, who had worked at Fiat and Enfield-Allday. Renwick had inherited a huge fortune, and when Renwick & Bertelli Ltd was formed, its first project was a 1.5-litre single-overhead-camshaft engine. For testing purposes, this was mounted in an Enfield-Allday chassis with bodywork designed by Bertelli's brother, Enrico. The car played a key role in Aston Martin's immediate future and went on to be known as 'Buzzbox'.

After visiting Aston Martin's Kensington premises and meeting Benson, Renwick and Bertelli recognised that investing in a known marque rather than trying to establish their own would give their ambitions a headstart. When the deal was done, Aston Martin moved a few miles south-west from Kensington to new premises at Victoria Road in Feltham. The building was previously used to build Whitehead aircraft, and Enrico Bertelli set up shop next door. His coachwork would grace Astons for years to come.

Although it was the beginning of a new era for the company, it would still be some time before Aston Martin was on any sort of relatively secure footing. Even so, in 1927 it had three cars on its Motor Show stand – saloon and tourer versions of the new T-type, plus a more sporting short-chassis prototype with an underslung chassis. All featured the Renwick and Bertelli 1.5-litre four-cylinder engine, but the T-types were heavy, expensive and underpowered. It quickly became clear that

Robert Bamford served in the Royal Army Service Corps during World War One, and would leave Aston Martin shortly after the nascent company got going again following hostilities. *AMHT*

Aston Martin's future lay far more with the sports car.

Bertelli, like Lionel Martin before him, was acutely aware of motorsport's value in terms of both developing and promoting his cars. In 1928, the company therefore made its first appearance at the Le Mans 24 Hours, Bertelli sharing one car – LM1 – with George Eyston, while Jack Besant and Cyril Paul shared LM2. Both Astons retired, but it was the beginning of a long and successful relationship with the endurance classic.

That 1927 Motor Show prototype formed the basis for the Sports Model, which would morph into the International, but first Benson and Charnwood left the company then, in 1931, Renwick also departed. Two years previously, Sidney Whitehouse had invested in Aston Martin and come on board

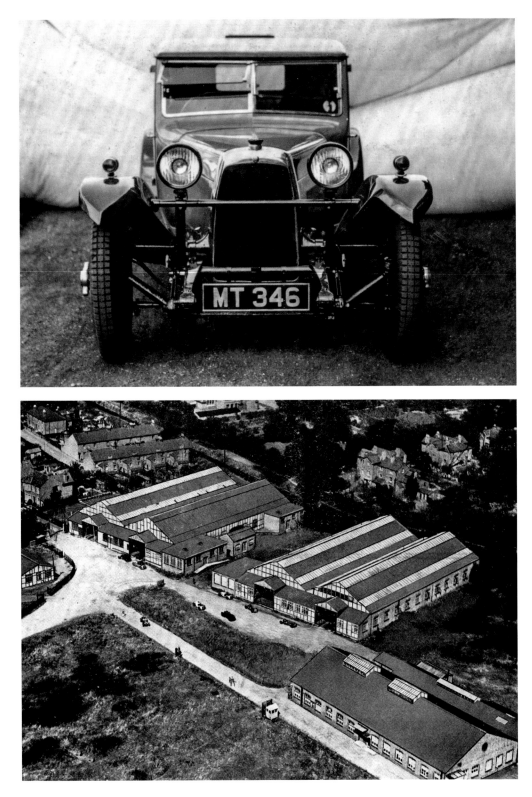

as chairman, and in 1931 a wealthy enthusiast by the name of Lance Prideaux-Brune provided further financial backing.

A heavily redesigned 'Second Series' chassis was introduced late that year. The company had built 132 First Series cars, including five more team cars. LM3 and LM4 were raced at the Brooklands Double Twelve – *Motor Sport* noting of the inaugural 1929 event that 'the unsupercharged Aston Martin put up a really wonderful performance' – and the Irish Grand Prix, while LM3 also appeared in the Tourist Trophy at Ards.

LM5, LM6 and LM7, meanwhile, featured an improved cylinder head among many other modifications, and these later First Series cars continued to appear at all of the major meetings, from Brooklands to the Tourist Trophy and Le Mans. All seven of the First Series team cars survive.

The Second Series cars featured a chassis designed by Claude Hill that was much simpler than its predecessor. In a further attempt to save costs, various components were bought in for the first time, such as the Laycock gearbox and the ENV rear axle. By far the most successful of this generation was the Le Mans, a rakish model that was named in honour of the class win – and fifth overall – that had been achieved by Bertelli and Maurice Harvey in the 1931 running of the 24 Hours.

Sammy Newsome and Henken Widengren would repeat that result in 1932, and their car was subsequently driven at Shelsley Walsh. 'With many of the cars in an apparently hopelessly unready state,' wrote the *Motor Sport* correspondent, 'the proceedings were opened by a demonstration run by AC Bertelli on the Aston Martin which had gained such magnificent honours at Le Mans the previous week. Using an 8 to 1 bottom gear, Bertelli made a very useful climb, and was handsomely cheered by the crowd as he ascended the hill.'

Behind the scenes, there were yet more changes. In 1932, Sir Arthur Monro Sutherland, a Newcastle shipping magnate,

■ Above left: the Martin-era road cars were powered by a sidevalve engine and built in tiny numbers. When Renwick and Bertelli took over, the company moved to Feltham (pictured left and right).
AMHT

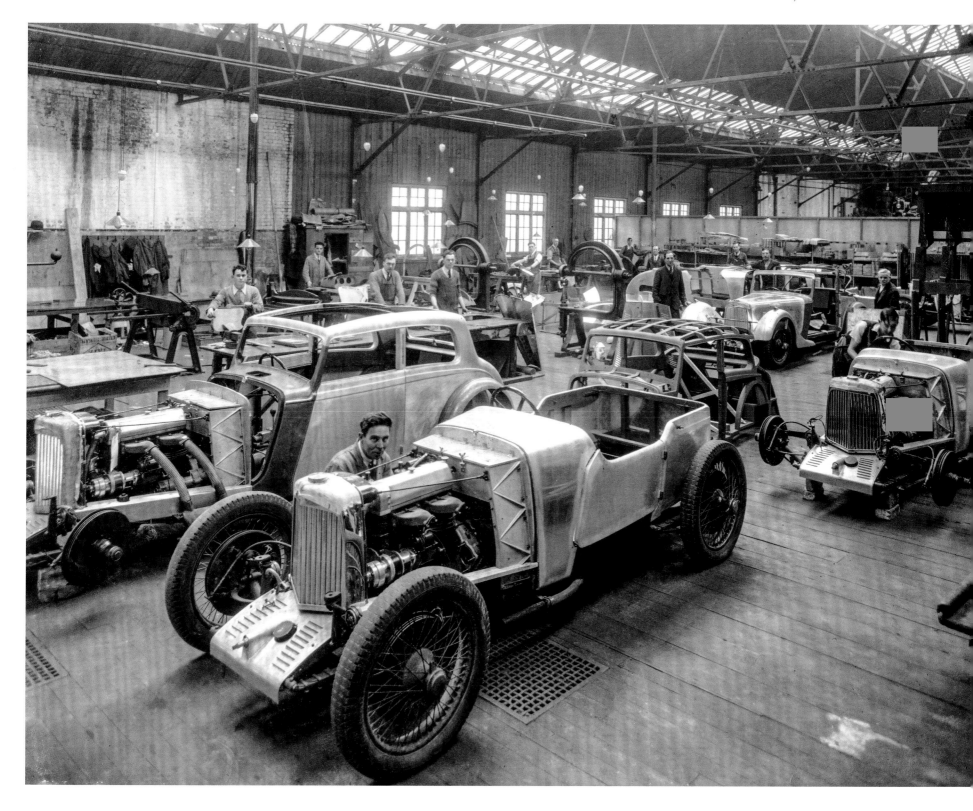

Aston Martin's Le Mans model was named after its class win in the 1931 Le Mans 24 Hours, delivered courtesy of Bertelli and Harvey. *AMHT*

Three works cars – LM11, LM12 and LM14 – were entered for Le Mans, but weren't able to repeat the success of previous seasons. The leading Aston was a privateer entry that finished 10th overall in the hands of Reggie Tongue and Maurice Faulkner, but there was much better to come in September's Tourist Trophy, which was held on the Ards road circuit in Northern Ireland. After more than six hours' racing, LM15, LM16 and LM17 crossed the line third, sixth and seventh to claim the Team Prize at this gruelling and prestigious race.

To celebrate the result, the two-seater sports version of the Mark II became known as the Ulster. It remains perhaps the most famous pre-war Aston Martin, and Bertelli considered it to be the best car he ever made.

In 1935 came more success at Le Mans, when the Ulster driven by Charles Martin and Charles Brackenbury – LM20, part of the latest run of team cars – finished third overall, won its class, and claimed both the Index of Performance and the Rudge-Whitworth Biennial Cup. Although sales had been strong in 1934 thanks to the introduction of the Mark II, they tailed off again in 1935 and Sutherland increasingly came to the realisation that building tiny numbers of expensive competition-based cars was not a sustainable business model.

The solution was a new Claude Hill-designed 2-litre engine, which was first fitted into a racing-orientated short-chassis Speed Model. The intention was for this to form the basis of a more comfortable and practical long-chassis production car – with yet more bought-in parts bringing down the cost and the majority wearing Enrico Bertelli saloon bodywork.

It quickly became apparent that the closed car was not going to be a success, though, and Aston Martin cut short its order from Enrico in order to focus production on open cars that would use the Speed Model's shorter chassis. As a result of this upheaval, 'Bert' Bertelli resigned but Sutherland pressed on with the revised 15/98 – which would make use of a further increased number of proprietary components – and Claude Hill stepped up to take overall charge of future designs.

It was Hill who would bridge the gap between the Bertelli cars and the David Brown era. While the 15/98 saw the company through to the outbreak of World War Two – during which the factory would be kept very busy, mostly making aircraft components – in the meantime Hill worked on some fascinating prototypes. One was christened 'Donald Duck' due to its ungainly looks and was based on the first 2-litre saloon. Its bodywork was removed in January 1938 and a new structure

invested in Aston Martin and became the new chairman. His son – Robert Gordon Sutherland, who was then only in his mid-20s – became the joint managing director. Sutherland Jnr's brief was to look after the business side of things while Bertelli focused on engineering. Amongst all of the distractions, Aston once again secured fifth overall at Le Mans in 1933, this time courtesy of Pat Driscoll and Clifton Penn-Hughes.

Such were the lessons being learnt by Bertelli during his competition outings that development of the company's production cars continued at breakneck speed. In 1934 came another new chassis from Hill, plus a new block and cylinder head for the 1.5-litre engine. Work had started on what became known as the Mark II during 1933, but its introduction was delayed slightly to enable the remaining stock of previous-generation Le Mans to be cleared.

This would be a busy and successful year for Aston Martin.

built up using square-section tubing, to which the steel panels were then attached. Various mechanical specifications were tried throughout 1938 and '39, and the car was timed at 90mph during tests at Brooklands.

Of far more long-term significance was the streamlined Atom that followed. This remarkable car appeared in July 1940, just as the Battle of Britain was breaking out. Developing the theme started by 'Donald Duck', the Atom used a square-section steel spaceframe with aluminium panels, independent front suspension, a Cotal electromagnetic gearbox and, initially, the 15/98's 2-litre engine. Sutherland and Hill tested the car extensively during the war, and by 1944 it had been fitted with Hill's new 1,970cc pushrod engine.

The Atom pointed the way towards Aston Martin's future but, although wartime work had put the company on a sound financial footing, Sutherland recognised that making the new

'The two-seater sports version of the Mark II became known as the Ulster – Bertelli considered it his best car'

Claude Hill's Atom may not have been the prettiest Aston Martin ever made, but it is certainly one of the most significant, and helped paved the way for the marque's post-war success. *AMHT*

'four' that the company scored one of its most significant racing successes. St John Horsfall and Hill persuaded Brown to let them prepare a car for the 1948 Spa 24 Hours at very short notice, but it outlasted the opposition – which included Luigi Chinetti's Ferrari 166 – to take victory. The weekend was also notable for the fact that Brown noticed how efficiently Dudley Folland's pit was being operated; the man in charge of it was called John Wyer.

The Spa winner was displayed at that year's London Motor Show alongside the 2-Litre Sports, which was based around the Atom chassis and became the first production car of the David Brown era. Retrospectively dubbed the DB1, only 14 would be built before Aston Martin really set the template for the next decade or so with the DB2. That car was previewed in a trio of 1949 racers that contested the Le Mans 24 Hours. Based on a shorter version of the DB1's steel frame and wearing curvaceous Frank Feeley-designed aluminium bodywork, two were fitted with the four-cylinder engine and one with the 2.6-litre Lagonda 'six'. Claude Hill was dismayed to learn that the Lagonda engine was being used when he was working on a six-cylinder version of his own powerplant, and left the company after a huge row with Brown.

With production of the DB2 getting under way in 1950, Aston Martin's racing commitment stepped up a notch and John Wyer was brought in to take care of its competition programme – Brown later described it as a temporary measure that lasted for 13 years. The DB2 was available in standard 107bhp form or as the 123bhp Vantage, and the works racers featured only minor modifications from the most potent roadgoing models.

At Le Mans that year, three cars were entered by the factory, wearing the now-famous registration numbers of VMF 63, VMF 64 and VMF 65. George Abecassis and Lance Macklin were entrusted with VMF 64 – they finished fifth overall, won their class and claimed the Index of Performance. It was a fine indication of the DB2's abilities and truly established its GT credentials, as did a one-two-three class result in September's Tourist Trophy at Dundrod.

The following year, VMF 64 – by then fitted with an aluminium cylinder head and triple Weber carburettors – finished third overall at Le Mans. It had been joined at La Sarthe by two lightweight DB2s that had been specially prepared for the 24 Hours – they finished fifth and seventh. Those versatile works DB2s were very much in the spirit of the later DB4 G.T., but from the end of 1951 onwards the development of road and

car a production reality would involve considerable investment – certainly more than he was prepared to put in. He therefore took the novel approach of putting the company up for sale via an advertisement in *The Times*.

One of those to express an interest was David Brown, from the eponymous family gear company. Sutherland was attracted to Brown's engineering credentials, and Brown was impressed by the Atom when he drove it, but his initial offer of £14,000 caused a degree of surprise given that the company's assets alone were valued at £21,000. In February 1947, they settled on £20,500, which Brown paid from his own personal fortune. Later that year, he added Lagonda to his portfolio, to a large extent because it gave him access to that marque's WO Bentley-designed, twin-overhead-camshaft, six-cylinder engine.

Like Bertelli and Bamford before him, Brown knew that motorsport could 'improve the breed' and provide valuable promotion, and considered that the Aston chassis with the Lagonda engine would form a potent combination both on and off the race-track. And yet it was with Hill's humble 1,970cc race cars started to go in very different directions.

At the end of 1950, Eberan von Eberhorst had been brought in as chief engineer and tasked with creating the competition-focused DB3. He came up with a new tubular chassis that housed a de Dion rear end and torsion-bar suspension, and initially the 2.6-litre engine was retained.

Certainly at first, the DB3 was not a conspicuous success. David Brown considered von Eberhorst to be too cautious in his approach, and the retirements mounted up during the first half of the 1952 season. A 3-litre version of the straight-six was particularly unreliable to begin with, and at Le Mans transmission troubles accounted for two of the three entries. Eventually, Aston Martin got on top of the various problems, and in August there was a welcome boost when Peter Collins and Pat Griffith won the Goodwood Nine Hours.

Over the winter of 1952-'53, Willie Watson designed a new, lighter chassis that retained many of the DB3's mechanical components but which was clothed in a heavily sculpted body by Frank Feeley. This was the DB3S, which did sterling service in various forms for the works team until its focus switched to the DBR1. In 1953, Reg Parnell finished fifth on the Mille Miglia – the best result that Aston achieved in an event that David Brown dearly wanted to win – but won the British Empire Trophy on the Isle of Man and the Goodwood Nine Hours with Eric Thompson. Collins and Griffith, meanwhile, won the prestigious Tourist Trophy at Dundrod. At Goodwood as well as the TT, the Astons beat a full complement of works Jaguar C-types, while in 1955 and '56 a DB3S was runner-up at Le Mans.

In road-car terms, the DB2 was replaced by the DB2/4 in 1953, Feeley's elegant lines being stretched to turn it into a 2+2 and its practicality being further boosted by the addition of a hatchback-style opening rear panel. The new model initially used its predecessor's Vantage-spec engine, but in 1955 a MkII DB2/4 was introduced with an enlarged 2.9-litre version of the straight-six.

That was also the year in which Wyer – who'd been promoted to technical director – officially separated the design of racing cars and production cars by creating new departments for each. Von Eberhorst had left at the end of 1953, and Wyer's reshuffle put Ted Cutting in charge of Aston Martin's racing designs, while Harold Beach would oversee road-car engineering. In terms of the latter, there would be one further development of the DB2 line – the DB MkIII, which was introduced in 1957. Donald Hayter styled an elegant front end that was lower and sleeker

Peter Clark and Mike Keen finished seventh overall at Le Mans in 1952, driving their privately entered DB2. *AMHT*

than that of its predecessor, while new recruit Tadek Marek made improvements to the 2,992cc engine.

Larger valves and higher-lift camshafts were fitted, the block was made stiffer and the crankshaft was stronger. Over the course of DB MkIII production, it would be available in various states of tune: there was the 162bhp 'DBA' with twin SU carburettors; the 'DBD' with triple SUs and 180bhp; and the 'DBB' with triple Webers, a higher compression ratio, twin exhausts and 195bhp. The model also featured Girling front disc brakes.

By the time of the DB MkIII's launch, work was well under way on the replacement for a Feltham generation of cars that owed so much to Claude Hill's chassis, WO Bentley's Lagonda engine and David Brown's vision. Harold Beach had started Design Project 114 as early as 1954, but in its early stages – as we'll see later – it wasn't the revolutionary leap forward that it would eventually become.

By mid-1957, however, it had morphed into what we now recognise as the DB4. The first prototype to be bodied by Italian

The start of a new era for Aston Martin – the Touring-bodied DB4 was a marked departure from previous road cars, and caused a sensation when it was launched in 1958. *AMHT*

coachbuilder Touring – DP184/1 – arrived at Feltham in July and received its engine and transmission. The work was finished on a Saturday afternoon and Beach immediately took the car on a road-test, heading south-west from Feltham towards Chertsey. Almost exactly 60 years later, this sort of weekend shakedown of a new car would be repeated at Newport Pagnell with PP1 – the prototype for the DB4 G.T. continuation series.

The morning after that exploratory drive, Beach was joined by John Wyer and they drove DP184/1 up to David Brown's farm in Buckinghamshire. With Brown driving, the three men went out for an enthusiastic blast around the Chiltern hills, and the marque patron could immediately see the promise in this new design.

Wyer and his wife then took the prototype on a long European tour, covering 2000 miles and taking in a visit to Touring in Milan. Apart from a hair-raising problem with

the brakes, which faded almost to nothing while crossing the Vosges mountains, there were few serious mechanical problems and Wyer's report stated that 'the car has magnificent performance and is full of potential'.

When the DB4 was finally introduced to the public in October 1958 – at first the Paris and then the London motor shows – it caused a sensation. Distributors from around the world told Wyer that they'd be able to sell as many as Aston Martin could build, and its proven ability to go from 0-100mph-0 in less than 30 seconds made it one of the world's fastest cars.

With Aston Martin at that time being very much at the forefront of sports car racing, and now having this potent new Grand Tourer in its armoury, people naturally started to enquire almost immediately about the possibility of the company producing a competition variant. In that respect, John Wyer was ahead of the game.

The man behind the initials

The dapper Brown secured Aston Martin's future in the post-war years, and the company thrived under his direction. *AMHT*

D avid Brown was born into the family business. Literally, in fact – he arrived into the world in Park Cottage, the Browns' home and, for a time, part of the site on which their gear-making company would flourish. Established in 1860 by David's grandfather – who was also called David – it was originally based in a stable block in Huddersfield, West Yorkshire. By the time that the younger David Brown joined it in 1921, it employed more than 1000 people and had moved to the Park Works, still in Huddersfield and still, to this day, its UK base.

David's father Frank had taken over from the company founder and, worried that his son wasn't picking up the required knowledge to do likewise, sent David to Huddersfield Technical College. The youngster had well and truly been bitten by the motoring bug, travelling to the Park Works on a 1,000cc Reading Standard motorcycle and even working on his own design of car – he cast the cylinder block for its straight-eight while working in the foundry – before Frank put a stop to it. He raced, too, first on the Reading and then with a TT Vauxhall that was given to him in bits by Amherst Villiers, who had approached the company to manufacture his superchargers.

Such frivolities were curtailed when, at the age of just 29 and having spent time working in each area of the company in order to gain a proper grounding in it, David was put in charge of its day-to-day running. A dynamic and tenacious man, he established a new foundry in Penistone in 1936 then – three years later – set up a tractor division after an earlier partnership with Harry Ferguson had fallen apart. Its manufacturing plant was in Meltham, a site that played a key role in the construction of post-war Aston Martins until the company became established in Newport Pagnell.

Frank died in 1941 and David acquired complete control of the business. Having bought Aston Martin following the war, he oversaw the rebirth of the marque, its racing success and the development of the famous DB line of cars. And yet it's said that his proudest achievement of the 1950s was one of his horses – Linwell – winning the 1957 Cheltenham Gold Cup. An accomplished rider, he was master of the Badsworth and South Oxfordshire hunts.

In 1960, David Brown Ltd's gear, foundry and tool divisions were organised into one company, with Aston Martin and Tractors remaining separate. After presiding over years of unprecedented growth, harsh reality set in during the early 1970s and both Aston and the tractor division were sold in 1972. It was a tough decade for the parent company and, having moved to Monte Carlo in 1977, Brown eventually sold up in 1990.

Photographs of him from his Aston Martin days always show him to be immaculately turned out, and while he worked hard he still found time to enjoy the finer things in life – and he remained a motoring and motorsport enthusiast throughout. The man who played such a key role in the long history of Aston Martin died in 1993.

Chapter 2
THOROUGHBRED RACER

The years between 1959 and 1963 were a golden period for GT racing, and Aston Martin fired the opening salvo with the DB4 G.T. Not long afterwards came the Ferrari 250GT SWB, followed in 1961 by the Jaguar E-type. Development was frantic: first the Aston gained lighter bodywork and a more powerful engine for the Zagato variant, then came the even more specialised Project cars. Ferrari returned fire via the 250GTO and Jaguar via the Lightweight E-type, not to mention Carroll Shelby joining the party with his new Cobra.

For a time, it even looked as if the World Sports Car Championship would be contested solely by GT cars, this being part of a cyclical identity crisis through which sports car racing regularly puts itself. In a nutshell, the machinery involved gradually gets further and further away from recognisable road cars – more expensive and more specialised – until manufacturers and entrants start to question its relevance and the 'reset button' has to be pressed.

In the end, that reset didn't entirely happen during the early 1960s. Instead, sports-racing prototypes continued to race alongside the GTs, which from 1962 would be contesting the International Championship for GT Manufacturers but stood little chance of overall victory in the biggest races.

David Brown himself addressed this subject as early as October 1959, at a dinner held ahead of that year's London Motor Show. He pointed out that the latest sports-racing cars had become 'a more complicated and expensive version of a Grand Prix car' and went on to question the purpose of sports car racing. His own preference was for it to feature models that had a degree of relevance to those that the general public could buy, and announced that for 1960 Aston Martin would be withdrawing from sports car competition and concentrating upon Grand Prix racing with its DBR4.

It helped, of course, that in 1959 Aston Martin had achieved its greatest ambition and pipped Ferrari and Porsche to the world championship with Ted Cutting's gorgeous DBR1. That year, the season comprised only five races and, of those, John Wyer had initially decided to enter just the Le Mans 24 Hours – and even that was only due to pressure from David Brown. There was a point at which thought was given to not going sports car racing at all in '59.

As it turned out, Wyer was persuaded to send a car for Roy Salvadori and Carroll Shelby to drive in the opening round at Sebring, but they were forced to retire when the gearlever broke off in the latter's hand.

Ferrari took full marks in Florida, with Porsche doing likewise on the Targa Florio, which Aston Martin didn't enter. On 7 June, however, the incomparable Stirling Moss ignited the firm's challenge with an epic victory in the Nürburgring

Phil – you were the first human being to finish.'

As Wyer later wrote, 'And so to Le Mans'. Three cars were entered: chassis DBR1/3 would act as the hare and be driven by Moss and Fairman; DBR1/2 was for Salvadori and Shelby; and DBR1/4 was for Maurice Trintignant and Paul Frère. They would be up against a trio of works Ferrari 250 TRs and three potentially giant-killing factory Porsche 718 RSKs.

Denis Jenkinson would later write in *Motor Sport* that Aston's victory came about thanks to 'reliability, careful planning, coolness and discipline which was a fine example of how to approach the Le Mans 24-hour race'. The team certainly had a better grasp of strategy than the Ferraris, which were goaded into chasing Moss's leading car during the early hours and then tackled pitstops in a chaotic fashion that stood in direct contrast to Aston Martin's efficient approach.

Eventually, the Moss / Fairman DBR1 retired with engine trouble, but the Ferraris then started to have problems of their own – first the Cliff Allison / Hermano de Silva Ramos car fell by the wayside, then the Dan Gurney / Jean Behra entry did likewise. By late on Sunday morning, the Hill / Gendebien Ferrari was in the lead; the remaining DBR1s – which had been carefully biding their time – were up to second and third.

Shortly after 11am, the Ferrari came into the pits with an overheating engine and, after a few further checks followed by some careful laps, the problem was diagnosed as being terminal. The Astons were through and swept to a famous one-two, Salvadori and Shelby delivering the victory that David Brown wanted above all others.

With Aston Martin now trailing Ferrari by only two points, the deciding race in the championship would be the Tourist Trophy at Goodwood on 5 September. Moss shared with Salvadori, Fairman with Shelby, and Trintignant with Frère as Aston launched a full-on assault on the historic race. On this occasion, Maranello had no answer and the biggest obstacle to a home victory was the fire that consumed the Aston Martin pit.

Moss, as usual, had dashed away at the start, with Shelby following. The first round of driver changes went without incident – Aston was benefitting from the fitment of pneumatic built-in jacks to the DBR1s. But when Salvadori came in to hand back to Moss, disaster struck. Fuel was gushing from the hose well before it was anywhere near the filler cap and soon ignited on the hot exhaust. Salvadori immediately leapt out with burning overalls, but then the refuelling tank collapsed and dumped yet more fuel over the area.

Moss pictured at Silverstone during the DB4 G.T.'s debut appearance in 1959 – he took a comfortable victory. *AMHT*

A superbly evocative shot of the winning DBR1 at Le Mans in 1959, the season in which the marque claimed the World Sports Car Championship. *AMHT*

1000km. After persuading Wyer to enter a lone DBR1 for him and Jack Fairman, Moss sprinted away from the Le Mans-style start and set a blistering pace to hand over to his co-driver with an enormous lead.

After six laps behind the wheel, Fairman slid off into a ditch and, while he was able to manhandle the car back on to the track and return to the pits, the Ferraris had got past, as had Umberto Maglioli's Porsche. Moss jumped back in and gave chase, retaking the lead and establishing an advantage that enabled him to stop and once more hand over to Fairman without surrendering the lead.

Fairman, however, was unable to hold off the charging Ferrari of Phil Hill and Olivier Gendebien, so during his final stint Moss had to do it all over again. He eventually crossed the line 41 seconds clear of the Ferrari, with the sister 250 TR of Tony Brooks and Jean Behra completing the podium in third. It was one of Stirling's greatest victories. Story has it that, after the race, Denise McCluggage said to Hill: 'Don't feel too badly,

Eventually the conflagration was brought under control and Moss was transferred to the Shelby / Fairman car. The drama had dropped it behind the Bonnier / von Trips Porsche, but Moss was soon back into a lead that wouldn't be relinquished. The best that Ferrari could do was third – after misunderstanding some late pit signals, Tony Brooks came within a whisker of catching von Trips for a second place that would have put Ferrari and Aston Martin equal on points, but the latter would still have taken the title courtesy of its three wins to Ferrari's one.

It is important to appreciate the significance of that 1959 season, during which the DBR1 secured its place in history and the DB4 G.T. made its debut. The balance of motor-racing power was slowly but surely shifting from Italy to Great Britain, and Aston Martin was at the very heart of that movement. The marque was rightly proud of it, too, the DB4 G.T. sales brochure including photographs of the DBR1's victories at the Nürburgring, Le Mans and Goodwood.

'In this year of triumphant Aston Martin achievement,' it stated, 'Aston Martin Lagonda Limited proudly announce the introduction of the David Brown Aston Martin DB4 G.T. Embodying the lessons of ten years of endeavour on the most arduous race circuits of the world, this new Grand Touring model is designed to provide for the most critical of high performance car owners a culminating experience of really fast motoring. Its performance is unique; its appearance and finish are immaculate; its behaviour is impeccable; it is eminently safe whether in competition or normal road usage… It has all functional elements to withstand the sustained high performance of which this car is capable.'

■ Above left: sadly, DP199 was an early retirement during the 1959 Le Mans 24 Hours. *AMHT*
Left: Innes Ireland hustling John Ogier's DB4 G.T. en route to third in the 1960 Tourist Trophy. *The Revs Institute / George Phillips*

The DB4 G.T. may have been officially unveiled in October 1959, but the prototype – DP199 – had actually made its racing debut months earlier. Its first appearance was at the Le Mans Test Weekend on 25-26 April, when it was driven by Swiss distributor Hubert Patthey and Renaud Calderari under the banner of Ecurie Trois Chevrons. Patthey managed to post the seventh-quickest time overall, while Calderari was 12th. Fastest in the Aston's 3-litre GT class, and fourth overall, was 'Beurlys' in a Ferrari 250GT that was entered by Equipe National Belge.

One week later, Stirling Moss gave DP199 its race debut proper at Silverstone during the BRDC International Trophy meeting. The car's entry – as mentioned, well in advance of its official introduction, let alone its homologation – caused a certain amount of controversy. John Wyer even had to give the organisers written confirmation that it would go into production before it was accepted.

The Aston's main rivals were John Coombs' Jaguar Mk1 – to be driven by Roy Salvadori – plus a works Lotus Elite for Colin Chapman, and Jack Sears was present in his rapid Austin-Healey 100-Six. There was also a smattering of Morgans and MGAs, but no one was a match for Moss. His pole-position time of 1m 55.4s was *five seconds* clear of Salvadori, who himself was only 0.8s ahead of the remarkable Chapman – a superb driver in his own right – aboard his diminutive Elite.

Predictably, Moss romped away when the flag dropped, later writing in his diary: 'Saloon race was easy. Used 5000rpm and won from Roy's 3.4. Jags were furious because car had a short wheelbase. Brakes could be better and I feel 700 tyres would help.' As the *Motor Sport* report later stated: 'Moss's 3.7-litre Aston Martin DB4 Coupe could hardly help winning…'

At both the Le Mans Test Weekend and Moss's Silverstone victory, DP199 had, as noted above, been fitted with a 3.7-litre engine – Wyer later stated that it featured a single-plug cylinder head – but when Patthey and Calderari returned to La Sarthe for the 24 Hours it had a detuned 3-litre DBR3 powerplant, albeit with the twin-plug head. Sadly, the engine lasted only 21 laps before expiring.

In November, Moss brought the DB4 G.T.'s maiden season to a close, this time at the wheel of the third production car – which had been prepared by the works but was owned by Frank de Arellano – in the agreeable surroundings of the Bahamas Speed Week. Moss won his heat at Nassau in chassis 0103 ahead of Salvadori's Healey 100S. He retired in the final, though, leaving John Cuevas to take victory in his Porsche.

For 1960, Aston Martin had officially withdrawn from sports car and GT racing in order to concentrate on Formula One, but it nonetheless produced a handful of lightweight DB4 G.T.s for privateers to race. Of those, Tommy Sopwith bought 0124 for his Equipe Endeavour outfit, while 0125 and 0151 went to John Ogier of the Essex Racing Stable, which benefitted from a great deal of factory support. Moss gave the Sopwith car a winning start at the Easter Goodwood meeting in front of an enormous crowd. In what would be one of his final DB4 G.T. outings, Moss once again trounced the Jaguar saloons in the 10-lap Fordwater Trophy, Salvadori and Sears trailing well behind.

For the rest of 1960, 0124 would mostly be campaigned by 'Gentleman Jack' Sears, and he took two wins in quick succession at Aintree and Oulton Park. He followed those races with an appearance in the 25-lap International Unlimited Sports-Car Race at the BRDC's Silverstone meeting, finishing 10th in a varied field that included Roy Salvadori's winning Cooper-Monaco, Jim Clark's Border Reivers Aston Martin DBR1 (which retired with a broken throttle linkage), a pair of Lister-Jaguars and no fewer than four Jaguar D-types.

In June, and with the DB4 G.T. by then officially homologated

Moss taking the Equipe Endeavour DB4 G.T. to victory in the Fordwater Trophy at the 1960 Easter Goodwood meeting. *LAT Images*

■ The Kerguen / 'Franc' Zagato
swings into Tertre Rouge ahead
of a diminutive DB and Abarth
during the 1961 Le Mans 24
Hours. The Aston retired almost
within sight of the finish.
LAT Images

a quartet of Ferrari 250GTs that were driven by Jo Schlesser, Wolfgang Seidel, Pierre Dumay and Mauro Bianchi. In the break between heats, Jenkinson noted of the DB4 G.T. that: 'After two hours of hard going, the engine looked as though it had come out of the showroom.'

The main event for 1960 was August's Tourist Trophy at Goodwood. No fewer than six 250GTs were entered, with Moss, Colin Davis and Dumay all being in the SWB model – as were the pairings of Seidel and Willy Mairesse, plus Graham Whitehead and Jack Fairman. Salvadori and Ireland were in Ogier's lightweight DB4 G.T.s, while the class was completed by a brace of Healey 3000s for Peter Riley and John Beckaert.

Moss made a lightning sprint across the track at the Le Mans-style start and led away – Mairesse, meanwhile, rather blotted his copybook by running to the wrong side of his Ferrari. Salvadori was always on good form for the TT and hung on to Moss in the early stages, then overtook him as the pair roared past the pits. It didn't last, the Ferrari slipping through again when Salvadori ran wide at St Mary's.

After that, it was Moss all the way and his eventual margin of victory at the end of the three-hour enduro was two laps. The Ferrari gained time during the pitstops because it only ever needed rear tyres, whereas Salvadori's Aston required new rubber all round at each stop apart from his final one – the DB4 G.T.'s final total for tyres used stood at 14, not helped by Roy also picking up a puncture. He nonetheless finished second, with Ireland third after a delay to reattach a trailing exhaust.

A crowd of some 60,000 enthusiasts watched as Jack Sears took the DB4 G.T. back to winning ways at Brands Hatch over the August Bank Holiday weekend. Sears won the opening race of the day, the 10-lap Wrotham Trophy, although he didn't have the strongest opposition around the Kent venue's fabulous Grand Prix layout. He set the fastest lap at 78.97mph and was followed home by Mike Parkes' Lotus Elite and Dick Gibson's modified Jaguar XK 120.

Development continued apace, and in October 1960 Aston Martin unveiled the muscular Zagato-bodied DB4 G.T. at the Earls Court Motor Show. Further weight-saving modifications were made for this latest variant, final assembly of which still took place in Newport Pagnell even if the bodies themselves were made by Zagato in Italy.

For the 1961 season, Ogier would acquire two of these Zagato-bodied cars – 0182 and 0183, famously known by their respective numberplates of 1 VEV and 2 VEV – while also

as a Grand Touring car, Jonathan Sieff raced 0125 at Rouen. The GP de Rouen was originally intended to be a Formula Two race, but organisers changed their mind at short notice, so a hotch-potch grid of sports cars and GTs was assembled. *Motor Sport* correspondent Denis Jenkinson loftily observed that: 'With such a wonderful circuit as that at Rouen-les-Essarts, it is a pity that the AC of Normandy could not use it for real racing cars.'

Still, there was a reasonable entry for the event, which would be decided by adding together the distance covered in a pair of two-hour heats. Jack Fairman took a predictably comfortable win in his DBR1, while Sieff twice got left behind at the Le Mans-style start and had to settle for sixth behind continuing to race 0151. In the earliest part of the season, Salvadori had an outing in the faithful 0125, finishing third at Snetterton behind the Ferrari 250GT SWBs of Mike Parkes and Graham Whitehead.

Come Easter Goodwood, though, it was Stirling Moss who put a Zagato DB4 G.T. – 0200, entered by Rob Walker and Dick Wilkins – on pole position for the 10-lap Fordwater Trophy. The meeting took place in poor weather, and even Moss struggled with the Aston during the race. Mike Parkes claimed victory in his Ferrari 250GT SWB, while on lap four Moss had a grassy excursion on the approach to St Mary's.

Three laps later, Innes Ireland got past at the same spot and went on cross the line in second place aboard the Touring-bodied 0151. Moss eventually finished third, and his day didn't improve in the Glover Trophy Formula One race – John Surtees held him off to take an impressive victory.

The week after Jean Kerguen and Claude le Guezec (in Zagato and Touring DB4 G.T.s respectively) had taken part in April's Le Mans Test Weekend, a new challenger appeared to take on the might of Aston Martin and Ferrari. Tommy Sopwith and John Coombs arrived at Oulton Park on 15 April with a Jaguar E-type apiece. Graham Hill took Sopwith's Equipe Endeavour car to victory, but Ireland managed to split the Jaguar duo by finishing second in 0151 – Salvadori, whose car was running out of brakes by the end of the race, was third in Coombs' E-type. The Ferrari 250GT SWBs of Jack Sears and Graham Whitehead had been outclassed, but it wouldn't take Maranello long to react to this new world order…

At the Le Mans 24 Hours, Ogier entered his two Zagato-bodied DB4 G.T.s: 0182 was to be driven by Jack Fairman and Bernard Consten, while 0183 was for the Australian duo of Lex Davison and Bib Stillwell. It didn't go unnoticed by the contemporary press that the Essex pit contained its fair share of Aston Martin employees and ex-works mechanics, but unfortunately both cars retired early with blown head gaskets.

The French-entered Zagato, 0180, being driven by Jean Kerguen and 'Franc', got rather further – to the 23rd hour, in fact – before failing to restart after a pitstop. It had been running ninth overall and was timed at 260kph on the Mulsanne Straight, only 5kph slower than the winning Ferrari TR/61 of Phil Hill and Olivier Gendebien.

After having to give best to Moss's Ferrari at the British Empire Trophy Meeting, Lex Davison had more success the following weekend in the GT support race for the British Grand Prix. The Australian drove 0183 for Ogier, and on the last of the 17 laps managed to find a way past Jack Sears in John Coombs' E-type. With Jaguar boss Sir William Lyons looking on, it must have been a particularly satisfying victory.

Ogier entered a formidable trio for August's Tourist Trophy at Goodwood: Roy Salvadori and Jim Clark were in 0182 and 0183 respectively, while Innes Ireland was in the Touring-bodied 0151. They would be up against the Ferrari 250 SWB pair of Stirling Moss and Mike Parkes, and in his autobiography *Jim Clark At The Wheel*, the Scot would later described his outing as 'a real tonic and I thoroughly enjoyed this race'.

Moss was fastest on the first day of practice with a time of 1m 34.8s, and such was his confidence that he then flew up to Morecambe before the end of Friday's session to switch on the town's illuminations! Parkes took advantage and snatched pole position with a lap that was 0.4s faster. Salvadori was the quickest of the DB4 G.T.s with a time of 1m 36.6s.

In the race, Parkes and Moss took a one-two for Maranello, despite the best efforts of the third-placed Salvadori – always something of a TT specialist. The Aston Martins were again harder on their tyres, but Clark finished fourth and Ireland fifth, which meant that Essex claimed the team prize.

In September, Tony Maggs scored another strong result in 0182, taking second behind Pierre Noblet's Ferrari in the Coppa Intereuropa at Monza – Kerguen was fourth in 0180. Both Maggs and Kerguen also appeared in the following month's Paris 1000km at Montlhèry, the former sharing 0183 with Sir John Whitmore and finishing ninth, the latter coming home 14th. Even the star pairing of Innes Ireland and Jim Clark could do no better than fifth aboard 0182.

The DB4 G.T. would be entering its third full season of racing in 1962, a year in which Carroll Shelby unveiled his Cobra and Ferrari introduced its latest 250 variant – the GTO. Aston Martin, meanwhile, responded with the first of its Project cars – the 212, which was developed by the factory for Le Mans that year – while Ogier continued to run 0182 and 0183. John Coombs covered nearly all of the available bases by acquiring the Zagato-bodied 0190 to go with his GTO and E-type, but sold the Aston Martin after Roy Salvadori had finished second in it at Brands Hatch in May – its sole outing with Coombs.

The previous weekend, Aston Martin itself had run 0183 at the Belgian Grand Prix meeting. Lucien Bianchi was hired to drive at Spa, and the car featured the magnesium-block 3,750cc engine that would go on to be used in the 1963 Project 214s. A

> **'The French Zagato was timed at 260kph on the Mulsanne, only 5kph slower than the winning Ferrari'**

young John Horsman – who eventually followed John Wyer to JWA when Wyer was tempted away from Aston Martin towards the end of 1963 – took it on a steady lap of the road circuit to warm it up and almost managed to go off at Les Combes due to the wet conditions.

He gathered it all up and later warned Bianchi to be wary of the tricky left-hander at the top of the hill, but seemingly to no avail. Shortly after taking the lead, Bianchi crashed heavily at the same spot. He walked back down to the pits and said that the team should be able to drive the car back after the race. They hiked up there only to discover that such was emphatically not the case. The car returned to Newport Pagnell, where it was completely rebuilt to the latest specification before being handed back to Ogier.

Neither of the two Zagato GTs that had been entered for Le Mans finished the race, and matters didn't improve at August's Tourist Trophy. Jim Clark and Chequered Flag boss Graham Warner were down to drive Ogier's cars – 1 VEV and 2 VEV – with Mike Salmon also entering a Zagato-bodied car.

Again, all three retired. Warner's car dropped out with a persistent misfire, Salmon's with gearbox trouble and Clark's due to an unfortunate coming-together with the race-leading Ferrari 250GTO of John Surtees. Clark had been struggling with the Aston's handling on a new set of tyres and was in the process of being lapped by Surtees when the car got away from him. Both were eliminated in the accident and Clark was mortified. Surtees was remarkably philosophical about it, simply saying: 'Well, that's motor racing.'

The Ogier Aston was rebuilt (again) in time for the Paris 1000km in October, but Clark and John Whitmore posted another DNF at Montlhèry due to a holed piston. There were some bright spots to be found in club meetings throughout 1962, but in the most prestigious races the season had been something of a disappointment.

By 1963, the Touring- and Zagato-bodied DB4 G.T.s had enjoyed their time in the sun and the main international events – Sebring, Le Mans, the Tourist Trophy – were being tackled by the new Project cars. But that's not to say that the earlier

variants disappeared altogether – far from it. Many went on to be enthusiastically raced in national meetings. The ex-Ogier 0125, for example, passed to Nick Cussons, who drove it during 1962 and early '63, and – as well being used on the road – it was still being entered in competitive events during the 1970s.

As values of original DB4 G.T.s rose through the 1980s, they were seen less and less in the cut and thrust of motorsport, but a run of much-modified and extensively lightened DB4s – built on standard long-wheelbase models – appeared during that decade and maintained the car's sporting presence.

More recently, the DB4 G.T. has become a mainstay of historic racing. At the 2011 Silverstone Classic, for example, the ex-Equipe Endeavour 0124 won the Royal Automobile Club Tourist Trophy for Historic Cars with Stuart Graham and Richard Attwood at the wheel. At the 2016 Goodwood Revival Meeting, the inaugural Kinrara Trophy – held for pre-1962 closed GT cars – featured no fewer than five DB4 G.T.s, one Zagato being joined by four Touring-bodied examples. No doubt John Wyer and David Brown would have very much approved.

Major race results 1959-'63

1959

DATE	VENUE	DRIVER/S (CHASSIS)	RESULT
2 May	Silverstone	Stirling Moss (DP199)	1
20-21 June	Le Mans	Hubert Patthey / Renaud Calderari (DP199)	Rtd
29 November	Nassau	Stirling Moss (0103)	DNF

1960

DATE	VENUE	DRIVER/S (CHASSIS)	RESULT
18 April	Goodwood	Stirling Moss (0124)	1
30 April	Aintree	Jack Sears (0124)	1
7 May	Oulton Park	Jack Sears (0124)	1
14 May	Silverstone	Jack Sears (0124)	10
22 May	Snetterton	Jack Sears (0124)	1
12 June	Rouen	Jonathan Sieff (0125)	6
1 August	Brands Hatch	Jack Sears (0124)	1
20 August	Goodwood	Roy Salvadori (0125)	2
		Innes Ireland (0151)	3
27 August	Brands Hatch	Jack Sears (0124)	2
23 October	Montlhèry	Innes Ireland / Roy Salvadori (0125)	6
		Jim Clark / Tony Maggs (0151)	DNF

1961

DATE	VENUE	DRIVER/S (CHASSIS)	RESULT
12 March	Sebring	Bob Grossman / Duncan Black (0133)	DNF
		Sherman Decker / Bob Bucher	DNF
25 March	Snetterton	Roy Salvadori (0125)	3
3 April	Goodwood	Innes Ireland (0151)	2
		Stirling Moss (0200)	3
15 April	Oulton Park	Innes Ireland (0151)	2
11 June	Le Mans	'Franc' / Jean Kerguen (0180)	DNF
		Jack Fairman / Bernard Consten (0182)	DNF
		Lex Davison / Bib Stillwell (0183)	DNF
8 July	Silverstone	Lex Davison	3
9 July	Charade	Jean Kerguen (0180)	DNF
15 July	Aintree	Lex Davison (0183)	1
		Sir John Whitmore (0151)	3
19 August	Goodwood	Roy Salvadori (0182)	3
		Jim Clark (0183)	4
		Innes Ireland (0151)	5
10 September	Monza	Tony Maggs (0182)	2
		Jean Kerguen (0180)	4
30 September	Snetterton	Innes Ireland	3

22 October	Montlhèry	Jim Clark / Innes Ireland (0182)	5
		Jean Kerguen / 'Franc'	14
		Tony Maggs / Sir John Whitmore	9

1962

DATE	VENUE	DRIVER/S (CHASSIS)	RESULT
7 April	Oulton Park	Tony Maggs (0182)	3
		George Pitt (0125)	-
		Mike Salmon	-
23 April	Goodwood	Mike Salmon	3
		Graham Warner (0182)	7
12 May	Silverstone	Jim Clark (0182)	4
		Mike Salmon	6
20 May	Spa	Mike Salmon	5
		Lucien Bianchi (0183)	DNF
25 May	Brands Hatch	Roy Salvadori (0190)	2
24 June	Le Mans	Jean Kerguen / 'Franc' (0193)	DNF
		Mike Salmon / Ian Baillie (0200)	DNF
18 August	Goodwood	Jim Clark (0183)	DNF
		Graham Warner (0182)	DNF
		Mike Salmon (0200)	DNF
21 October	Montlhèry	Jim Clark / John Whitmore (0183)	DNF

1963

DATE	VENUE	DRIVER/S (CHASSIS)	RESULT
15 April	Goodwood	Mike Salmon	5
11 May	Silverstone	Brian Hetreed	7
16 June	Le Mans	Phil Hill / Lucien Bianchi (DP215)	DNF
		Bill Kimberley / Jo Schlesser (0194)	DNF
		Bruce McLaren / Innes Ireland (0195)	DNF
		'Franc' / Jean Kerguen (0193)	DNF
30 June	Reims	Jo Schlesser (DP215)	DNF
7 July	Charade	Jean Kerguen (0193)	18
6 August	Brands Hatch	Innes Ireland (0194)	6
		Bill Kimberley (0195)	DNF
24 August	Goodwood	Bruce McLaren (0195)	DNF
		Innes Ireland (0194)	7
8 September	Monza	Roy Salvadori (0194)	1
		Lucien Bianchi (0195)	3
22 September	Montlhèry	Claude le Guezec (0194)	1
		'Franc' (0195)	2
6 October	Montlhèry	Jo Schlesser (0195)	1
		Claude le Guezec (0194)	5

The Project Astons

Innes Ireland rounds Woodcote in 0194 – one of two DP214s built – during the 1963 Tourist Trophy. *AMHT*

In terms of frontline motorsport, the last hurrah for the DB4 G.T. bloodline came courtesy of the short run of Project cars, which was the result of pressure from dealers – particularly Marcel Blondeau in France – for Aston Martin to officially return to motor racing. The first was DP212, which ran in the 4-litre Prototype class at Le Mans in 1962. Having been absent from competition for two years, Wyer treated the event more as a fact-finding mission than anything else – an initial toe in the water.

DP212 was closely based on the DB4 G.T. and retained its basic platform structure, which proved to be too heavy.

The engine was enlarged to 3,996cc, and while the front suspension shared the DB4 G.T.'s wishbones and coil springs, the rear gained a de Dion set-up plus torsion bars. The four-speed synchromesh gearbox was carried over, and a sleek new lightweight body designed.

The new Aston Martin was to be driven at Le Mans by Graham Hill and Richie Ginther. In his autobiography *Life At The Limit*, Hill described it as a 'jolly nice car' and commented on its speed through the fast right-hander after the pits. He did, however, state that there was noticeable rear-end lift at high speed – Ginther suggested fitting a spoiler, and one was subsequently tested at MIRA in September that year before being adopted for the 1963 Project cars.

Hill made a superb start at Le Mans and was actually leading at the end of the first lap. He later wrote that this temporary state of affairs was 'very stirring, especially for those connected with Aston Martin and all who hoped for a British victory'. Sadly, the obviously promising DP212 was delayed by dynamo problems before retiring with piston failure after 79 laps.

With Aston Martin having been suitably buoyed by DP212's performance, three more Project cars were built for 1963. The two DP214s were designed to run in the GT class and were therefore still – on paper, at least – closely related to the DB4 G.T. They were even given chassis numbers to suit – 0194 and 0195. The third was a more radical prototype designated DP215.

In reality, the DP214 and DP215 were both built around a completely new, much lighter, box-section frame. In this case of the DP214, even Wyer would later admit that this was blatantly against the rules, but correctly reasoned that no one would look too closely. The DP214s ran with 3,750cc engines, while the 215 had a dry-sump 3,996cc unit that allowed for a lower bonnet line. All three featured a Kamm-style tail with spoiler in order to reduce the rear lift from which DP212 had suffered.

While the DP214s employed the DB4 G.T.'s standard four-speed gearbox and Salisbury rear axle, DP215 had an independent double-wishbone rear with the CG537 transaxle that had caused problems in the DBR1 and would do so again here – it failed after 29 laps at Le Mans, where the car was driven by Phil Hill and Lucien Bianchi.

The two DP214s had been entrusted to Bruce McLaren / Innes Ireland and Bill Kimberly / Jo Schlesser, but both suffered from piston failure. Wyer later explained that supplier Hepworth & Grandage had designed forged pistons but time pressure forced it instead to use cast ones.

McLaren's engine blew on the Mulsanne Straight and unfortunately deposited its oil across the track. Roy Salvadori's Cunningham-entered Jaguar E-type was one of the first cars to come through and, after a brief struggle during which he thought he'd controlled the slide, the British ace suffered an almighty accident and was thrown clear. He survived with serious bruising, but Christian 'Bino' Heins was not so lucky when he also went off on the oil – his Alpine caught fire and he succumbed to his injuries.

First of the Project cars was DP212, seen here at the 1962 Le Mans 24 Hours, where it was driven by Graham Hill and Richie Ginther. *AMHT*

Schlesser subsequently drove DP215 in a support race for the French Grand Prix at Reims and led away in an event that he should have been able to win at a canter. Once again, however, the transmission gave trouble and Schlesser missed a few gearchanges, eventually bending the valves in the process.

The DP214s – now belatedly equipped with forged pistons – were entered for August's Tourist Trophy but were hamstrung by officialdom. The homologation form called for 5.5in wheels to be fitted, but at Goodwood the Astons arrived with the 6.5in rims that were necessary for Dunlop's latest tyre. They'd run at Le Mans in that spec without problem, but in West Sussex the scrutineer was having none of it, despite Wyer protesting that all the production cars were by then running the wider wheel.

It didn't wash. Innes Ireland and Bruce McLaren were allowed to practice on the 6.5in wheels but their times wouldn't count. As if to prove a point, Ireland matched the pole-position time of 1m 27s set by Graham Hill's Ferrari GTO. With the narrower rims fitted, and his times therefore counting towards the grid, he lined up third.

■ Final fettling for the Schlesser / Kimberly DP214 at Le Mans in 1963. The revised Kamm-style tail, with spoiler, is clearly visible and improved the car's high-speed aerodynamics. *AMHT*

McLaren ran solidly during the race before retiring with engine trouble, but Ireland was in a typically combative mood. Soon after the start, he split the Ferraris of Hill and Mike Parkes, then went off at Woodcote – taking Hill with him – while attempting to dive into the lead. Both men recovered, but the Aston was soon in to replace its flat-spotted tyres. A scurrilous rumour went around that the team had fitted the 6.5in wheels during the stop, with the result that the car was surrounded by officials when it next came in.

Although now a lap down, Ireland was soon running in company with the leading Ferraris. He was in no mood to say 'after you' and again went off at Woodcote, this time involving Parkes in the incident. The Aston later spun there for a third

time, all on its own. After a busy, and no doubt frustrating, afternoon in which he fought his way back up to fourth place only for the crew's jack to malfunction during the final pitstop, Ireland eventually crossed the line in seventh.

The next works outing for the DP214s came shortly after the Tourist Trophy. Both cars were entered for the three-hour Coppa Intereuropa, which took place at Monza during the Italian Grand Prix meeting. One was for Lucien Bianchi, the other was for Roy Salvadori – and it was 'Salvo' who gave the car a glorious victory.

Aston Martin engineer John Horsman got the axle ratio just right for the fast circuit and Salvadori revelled in the car's handling. He took things gently in practice, qualifying only

fourth, but come the race he was soon piling the pressure on the Ferrari GTO of race leader Mike Parkes. After the refuelling stops at half-distance, the two ran absolutely together, regularly swapping positions in a way that the pre-chicane Monza always seemed to encourage.

Knowing that he needed to build a slight advantage in order to prevent Parkes out-dragging him in the sprint from the final right-hander to the finish line, Salvadori took great risks while he was lapping traffic a couple of laps from the end and just about held on to take one of his most impressive victories. His overall race average was 120.23mph, and Bianchi provided the icing on the cake by finishing third.

The final works outing came with both DP214s at Montlhèry

on 6 October 1963. Fittingly, Jo Schlesser won the race from Jean Guichet's Ferrari 250GTO, with Claude le Guezec coming home fifth. The factory once again withdrew from official competition and Wyer left to join Ford's GT40 programme. David Brown later claimed not to be that keen on the Project cars. He considered them somewhat dated and would have preferred to return to racing with a cutting-edge mid-engined design, but nonetheless they kept the Aston Martin name at the forefront of GT racing for another couple of years.

Of Wyer, Brown had nothing but praise. During the full-time competition schedule of the 1950s that bought so much success, he'd simply left Wyer to get on with it. Theirs had been a truly formidable partnership.

Phil Hill and Lucien Bianchi drove DP215 at Le Mans in 1963. Although it failed to finish, it showed immense pace during practice, Hill lapping only 1.1 seconds slower than the pole-sitting Ferrari prototype.
LAT Images

Part 2
THE CONTINUATION PROJECT

Chapter 3
ON THE SHOULDERS OF GIANTS

Production of the Aston Martin DB4 lasted from 1958 until 1963, when it evolved into the DB5, which was launched at the Frankfurt Motor Show that September – the same month in which John Wyer left the company. And it was very much an evolution, the new car retaining the Superleggera construction – of which more anon – as well as the exterior lines of the later incarnations of DB4.

During the DB5's production run, all of the remaining Feltham activities – the departments for engineering and servicing were still based there – were transferred to the Newport Pagnell premises that David Brown had been developing following the acquisition of Tickford. The company even put on a bus service between the two sites during the transition period. With the M25 motorway having subsequently been built, it's now a distance of about 60 miles. How long it took during the mid-1960s sadly went unreported.

In 1965, the DB5 was replaced by the longer-wheelbase DB6, which featured a Kamm-style rear end that evoked the DB4-era Project racers. To many people, the trio of DB4, 5 and 6 still defines their idea of a classic Aston Martin, but by the late 1960s a fresh generation of cars was clearly needed. Tadek Marek's new 5.3-litre V8 was first seen in 1969 fitted to the DBS, which in turn morphed into the Aston Martin V8 – a model that would hold the fort through various financial crises and changes of ownership during the next 15 years or so.

The Newport Pagnell factory remained a constant, too. From the DB4 and the V8 to the Virage and the Vanquish, more than 13,000 cars left the famous works before UK production, design and engineering eventually moved to Gaydon in 2007. The final Vanquish – an S model, chassis number 502593 – rolled out of Tickford Street on 19 July.

But that's not to say that the site suddenly became dormant. Under the stewardship of Kingsley Riding-Felce, Aston Martin Works Service maintained the marque's presence in Newport Pagnell. One of the main buildings became Works Service itself, a facility that was able to look after Astons old and new, and which invested in apprentices to learn the necessary skills from older hands who might have built the cars in the first place.

In another building was the Heritage Restoration Centre, which took care of rebuilds, and in 2012 a modern new showroom was added with a huge glass wall, through which you can see what's going on in Works and, once it had been erected, the DB4 G.T. Build Centre. Crucially for the continuation project, all of this meant that the knowledge and ability into which the team would need to be tapping was still on-site. There was a body shop there, for a start, as well as all of the original tools and every build sheet.

Even so, restarting production of the DB4 G.T. at Newport

Left: a sad day as the last Vanquish leaves the line in 2007, signalling the end of production at Newport Pagnell. But thanks to the Heritage Centre (above), the site continued to thrive.

Pagnell – 10 years after that final Vanquish had rolled out, and more than 50 after the final DB4 G.T. – would not be a straightforward process. The continuation project was the brainchild of Paul Spires, President of Aston Martin Works. A man with an impressively wide array of talents, Spires raced Aston Martins, engineered cars at Le Mans and in the BTCC, and won 'bits and pieces' while both driving and acting as team manager. He joined the company in 2012 to set up the sales side of Aston Martin Works. When the esteemed Riding-Felce decided to retire, Spires took over.

But why choose to remanufacture the DB4 G.T.? Despite the standard DB4 being the first in a new generation of Aston Martin road cars, and the G.T.'s unquestioned competition pedigree, if you show a picture of either model to a member of the public and ask them what it is, chances are they'll say it's a DB5. Such is the power of a certain British secret agent and his enduring film franchise. But the DB4 G.T. has long been recognised by the *cognoscenti*, and Spires knew that the original Touring-bodied version would be the ideal candidate for his ambitious project.

'It's a forgotten hero, in my opinion,' he says. 'Most people gravitate towards the Zagato rather than the original-bodied car. I wanted to restart production [at Newport Pagnell], so I kind of wanted to turn back the clock to 1959. Also, because of modern homologation and legislation, we couldn't build a road car – we had to build a track car. The DB4 G.T. seemed like the ideal candidate because it was originally conceived as a track car. It's one of my personal favourites, too.

'Also, we should have built 100 for homologation purposes

The Heritage Centre has for decades been restoring classic Aston Martin models, which meant that some vital skills remained on-site.

in 1959 – we built 75. The rest of the balance was made up of specials and development cars to get us up to the 100. There was a gap of 25 cars there.'

The thorny issue of homologation – particularly surrounding exactly what constitutes, in competition terms, a GT car of any type – could quite easily fill a book on its own, but the facts surrounding period DB4 G.T. production are well known. The 75 Touring-bodied models were built between September 1959 and March 1963, although the vast majority had been completed by 1961. Their chassis numbers ran consecutively from DB4/GT/0101 to 0175.

The 19 Zagato-bodied cars used chassis numbers 0176 to 0191, plus 0193, 0199 and 0200. Chassis 0201, meanwhile, went to Italian coachbuilder Bertone. There it was fitted

with a sharp, flowing steel body that was styled by a young Giorgetto Giugiaro. Named Jet, the car was first shown at the 1961 Geneva Salon, and during the 1980s it was restored at Newport Pagnell.

Of the 'missing' DB4 G.T. numbers that remained unused, 0194 and 0195 were allocated to the two Project 214 racers during the early 1960s, while 0192, 0196, 0197 and 0198 were used by the Aston Martin-approved Sanction II Zagato-bodied cars that were built in the late 1980s. Logically enough, it was proposed that the 25 Touring-bodied continuation cars would use exactly the same format of chassis number, beginning at DB4/GT/0202 in order to carry on the original sequence.

'It took us quite a lot of time to gain everybody's confidence to allow us to do this,' remembers Spires. 'It's fraught with danger. Any car manufacturer takes their time to make very informed decisions. We finally got a decision in December 2016 to move forward with it and we moved forward at a real pace.'

One of the first jobs was to get the necessary suppliers and technical partners on board because there are two basic ways in which a manufacturer can approach a project such as this, one of which was never entertained by Aston Martin. It's actually the easier solution – make something that closely resembles a DB4 G.T. but with modern components underneath. Modern engine, modern switchgear, modern suspension, modern structure.

The other option makes life far more difficult – restart production exactly as it would have been almost 60 years previously, to the extent that you'd be hard-pressed to tell apart a DB4 G.T. that rolled out of Newport Pagnell in 1959 and one that did likewise in 2018. More challenging it may be, but it's the only way to genuinely and authentically honour the period DB4 G.T. – and it's the only route that Spires wanted to follow.

The original idea, in fact, was to make the 25 cars and then do a one-make championship with them. 'When we started talking to customers,' explains Spires, 'they were keen to take them on-track but were less keen to actually start racing them…'

Although that idea was therefore placed to one side, Spires and his team pressed on. It was decided that the continuation cars would be built to Lightweight specification, six of which had been constructed in period in order to keep the DB4 G.T. competitive in racing. Four were ordered as Lightweights and therefore built as such from the outset. These were chassis 0124 (registered 587 GJB and delivered new to Tommy Sopwith), 0125 (18 TVX, John Ogier), 0167 (a development car that would be registered 40 MT) and 0168 (which was exported to a New York dealer).

Two further cars were modified to Lightweight specification at Newport Pagnell during their build process – 0151 was registered 17 TVX and was another of John Ogier's racers, while 0175 wore the last Touring-bodied chassis number and was sold new to AG Medawar in Switzerland.

All six Lightweight DB4 G.T.s got their name via the extensive use of aluminium for the door frames, wheelarches, the upper section of the bulkhead, the floor panels, boot pan, bonnet and boot lid. The front crossmember was drilled, as were the front side rails and even the brackets for the Watt linkage and brake lines. The bumpers were deleted, one bonnet prop rather

Servicing for all ages of Aston Martin – even those built at Gaydon – is still carried out in the historic buildings.

than two was used, and there was no heater, radio, clock or glovebox lid. All of these were aspects that had to be taken into consideration, and going down the route of exacting authenticity meant that the people who would come together at Newport Pagnell in order to make it a reality had to be carefully selected.

'To assemble the team was difficult,' says Spires, 'because clearly you can't go and hire people who built the cars back in the day! It's a younger team and it's a very mixed skillset – there's a really good cross-pollination of skills that actually make the car the way it is. That worked extremely well, and there's been some good learning for everybody. I think they call it cross-functional working! There's been a lot of lessons learned.'

The famous Olympia building is one of the most recognisable landmarks at Newport Pagnell, and remains in use as an impressive showroom.

One of the first jobs in terms of personnel was to appoint a Programme Manager. Simon Hatfield had joined Aston Martin Lagonda in June 2014 as a Vehicle Engineering Leader, and it was he who would be entrusted with the engineering and delivery of the DB4 G.T.

'The project properly started in January 2017,' Hatfield explains. 'That's when we began to ramp it up. I was the second member on the team, and it's quite nice to know that we recruited the group that we've got around us – we've put together a really good bunch.

'We had loads of people apply and we tried to pick people from various backgrounds. We've got technicians who did their apprenticeship at Newport Pagnell and have always worked on Heritage cars, so they've got an understanding of how they go together and their little niggles. The artisan methods of building them – they know a lot about that.

'We've taken a couple of guys from the Heritage business who've been doing this for a long time, and they're great for how things go together – the "feel" elements such as wheel bearings. They take years of experience, learning how to set those up properly. There's a chap who's spent 25 years racing historic cars. He's been there and done it, and it's great to tap

into that knowledge. They're not normal technicians – I ask for more from them than that. They're not fitting Part A and Part B over and over again.'

With the team beginning to come together, it wasn't simply a case of raiding the stores at Newport Pagnell and starting to build DB4 G.T.s from an enormous stash of off-the-shelf components. It's one thing having enough spare parts on hand to restore or maintain existing cars – quite another to make an entire DB4 G.T. from scratch. The engineering challenge that they'd taken on was immense.

'There were a lot of things that, in effect, needed to be done in parallel,' says Hatfield of how they got started. 'We had to go and drag out the drawings that we had in the archive, we had to gather some [period] cars to get surface data from – the cars, and parts of the chassis, were hand-made and we knew that each one was slightly different.

'It's been very interesting to go and see all of these nice original race cars from different parts of the country and gather information from them. And it's lovely to look at the old drawings – you've almost got to use white gloves.'

That reference material was not the instant solution that you might expect, however: 'The amount of drawings that have

Paul Spires (right) was the driving force behind the continuation project, which was subsequently overseen by Simon Hatfield (below right).

got hand-written notes in the corner, and the writing's so bad you're not sure if it's someone's shopping list or whether it's relevant. Or it says, "See page two" and we've not got page two. We've had that quite a lot – we've got page one but we've not got pages two and three.

'It's nice to be able to use the old methods, but a lot of the parts have got no drawings at all. We've got 3,500 parts on the car and I've got a stack of 1,100 drawings, so I've got more than 2,000 bits in the middle that I've not got drawings for. A lot of those were just "bracket". A bracket was made and the holes were all slightly different. We've gone away from that and made every bracket the same.

'Loads of those parts were fixings, too. To a certain extent, a bolt's a bolt. As long as it's got the right pitch, the right thread, the right material strength, it doesn't need a drawing. Rivets – as long as it's the right material and the right strength and the right type, it's fine.

'There's probably 1,000 of those parts that are washers and spring washers, but we've gone from there. We could have put Nylocs on it, but originally it was a plain nut, a spring washer and a flat washer so we've done the same.'

Wherever there were gaps, inconsistencies and question

marks in the archive material, the team at Newport Pagnell had to do a lot of reverse engineering, using period components as a reference for making up a new drawing and subsequently getting that part remade. One considerable advantage in that respect was finding an owner of an original DB4 G.T. who allowed them to completely strip the car.

'If there's a part that we know we can buy, and it's a proven part, then we have done,' says Hatfield. 'Whereas things that don't exist anymore – such as engines and propshafts, all the body panels, all the interior – we've re-engineered it.'

They've also had to re-engineer parts that were available but which didn't come up to the required standard. A number of electrical components that were shared across many other cars during the 1950s and '60s are a case in point, Hatfield recalling one occasion when they ordered in a part and it arrived with 'Made in Egland' stamped on it.

'At that point,' he recalls, 'I realised that we needed to have a rethink and invest in the tooling. The scale of the task actually got bigger the more we looked into it.'

'Maybe naively,' adds Spires, 'when we started this we thought there were more parts that we could get off the shelf that would a) fit and b) be of a suitable quality. We found two things – they either didn't exist or the quality was not where we needed it to be.'

Rather than being viewed as obstacles, these challenges were enthusiastically embraced, and the knock-on effect that it had around Aston Martin Works and the company as a whole was immediately noticeable.

'A huge amount of people have seen it as a reflection of Works being a very forward-thinking, developing business,' explains Spires. 'We're not "just" the service centre, restoration centre and dealership that we've been for the past umpteen years – we've got some dynamic plans and expansion and new things going on.'

Far from being a one-off, it was also important that the continuation project brought a long-term benefit for Aston Martin, and the Newport Pagnell site in particular.

'We're trying to engage with the next generation,' says Spires. 'It's vital that we have good succession in the business, that we transfer the skills across from some of the older hands to the newer people because buildings are fantastic, but if you don't have the right skillset, then buildings are just buildings.

'There's been an enormous amount of learning. That's one of the nice things – it's developed those skills for the younger generation to come in and do this car. I'm not saying that they'd get lost but a lot of people involved with Heritage are getting older and we need to encourage the next generation. If they see a future with things like DB4 G.T., that encourages engineers and people to say, "That really excites me. Building a 1959 car from scratch – that's really something".

'It's an exciting programme, and perhaps making a new hot hatchback might not be as exciting to some engineers as coming to work here. Hopefully those people stay with Heritage and with Aston Martin and develop their skills. It's very important to me and to the business that in 60 years' time, people say, "That's a DB4 G.T. continuation car – I worked on those". It's a great piece of legacy for the business.

'It's always difficult to get the next generation engaged, and that's across the board – whether it's sales, service, parts, engineering. It's something that the UK car industry needs to work on. It needs a more cohesive plan.

'I'm very pro taking people that perhaps have fallen out of formal education and decided not to go to university – for whatever reason, they haven't got on with formal education but they've got very high skillsets in other areas. They could be making bodies for our cars, or engines – very hands-on and practical. I think in the UK we're missing a trick in terms of taking a lot of these very good, very disciplined people and moving them into other areas and other industries.

'The core skills in Heritage – being able to tune a carburettor, for example – we're losing. We need to not lose the young generation. We need to formalise a way to keep these key skills. We need to engage with them while they're at school, to show them a new direction.'

The DB4 G.T. continuation project offered the opportunity to harness and develop those skills, to create a showcase for Newport Pagnell and Aston Martin Works, and to celebrate one of the marque's most significant models.

'It was important to bring production back,' says Spires. 'It raised our profile massively within the business, whereas a lot of people said, "Newport Pagnell – didn't that close?" As far as they were concerned, it closed in 2007.

'And you'd be surprised how often people say, "Aston Martin don't do anything at Newport Pagnell anymore – they're at Gaydon". So I think it sends the message out there that we're very much alive and kicking.

'If you're a lover of the brand, you should be very proud that the company has allowed this to happen.'

There was a lot of archive reference material that the team could use, but still there were thousands of parts for which drawings didn't exist.

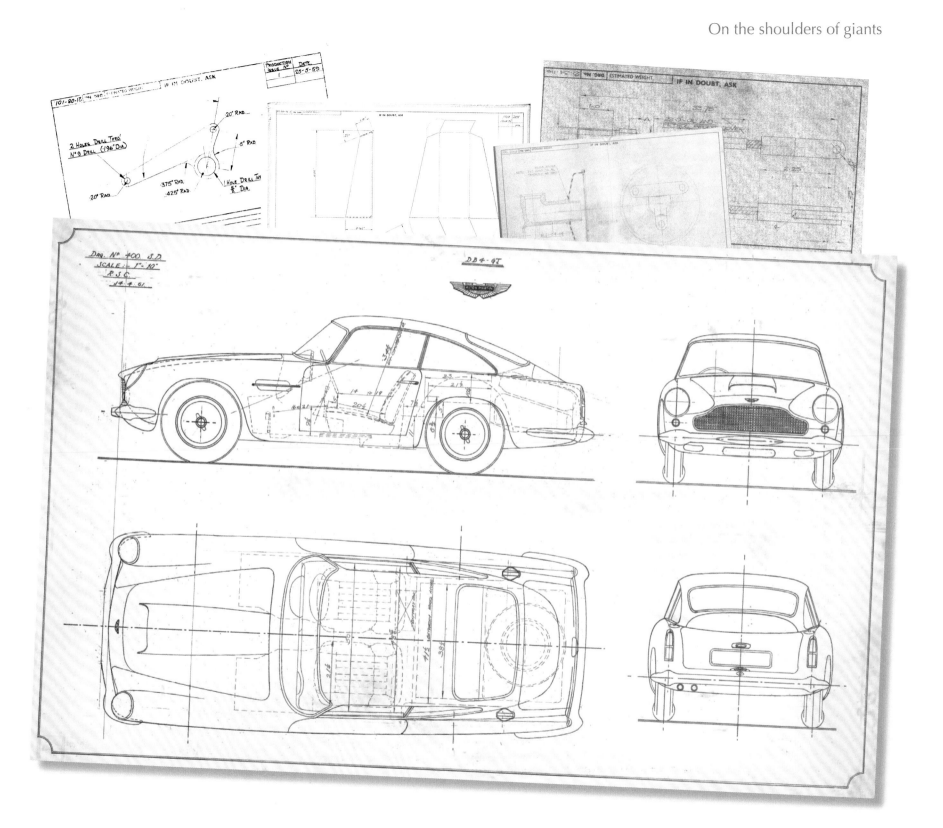

Aston Martin's historic home

The history of Aston's Newport Pagnell site can be traced to the first half of the 19th century. Joseph Salmons started his coachworks in the days of the horse-drawn carriage, and in 1844 bought the premises that he had previously been renting. He added to them as well, with new buildings that included a family house, which would later become offices.

The company was renamed Salmons and Sons in 1869 when Thomas and Joseph joined their father, and those two continued to expand the firm following his death in 1878. Business was clearly booming, in fact, with Salmons and Sons exporting its carriages around the British Empire – and the arrival of the motor car did nothing to change that. Thomas and

Joseph were quick to adapt to this new type of transport – their first car body was for a Daimler, in 1898 – and their employees were soon working overtime to keep pace with demand.

Salmons and Sons continued to grow in the early years of the 20th century, and it continued to be a family firm. Joseph's sons George and Lucas took over in 1909, the brothers living in respective halves of a semi-detached house called Sunnyside, which was next to the works. At that point, the company was producing hundreds of bodies each year, and in 1910 built the large three-storey workshop that still stands opposite Aston Martin Works. Two years later, 'Olympia' was added – the former showroom remains an important part of the Works site.

Salmons and Sons had made a name for itself in automotive terms via its all-weather bodies, first coming up with a spring-assisted hood then, in 1925, the so-called Tickford winding hood, which allowed owners to raise or lower the roof simply by cranking the handle. Two years previously, it had even introduced its own car – only 395 examples of the Meadows-engined NP were built, however.

During those inter-war years, Salmons built Tickford bodies for the likes of Vauxhall, Daimler, MG and Triumph, and in 1942 the company was renamed Tickford Ltd when manager Ian Boswell bought it from the Salmons family. Business showed no sign of slowing following WW2, with Tickford building bodies for, among a great many others, Healey and Alvis – the Coventry firm selected Tickford to produce the catalogued drophead coupé version of its Three Litre. It also made drophead coachwork for the Lagonda 2.6-Litre, plus coupé and drophead coupé variants of that car's successor – the 1953 3-Litre.

In 1954, David Brown bought Tickford as part of that decade's trend for traditional coachbuilders to be either bought outright by motor manufacturers or for exclusive supply deals to be struck up between them. It was one of the latter – between former Aston Martin supplier Mulliners and the Standard Motor Company – that provided much of the motivation for David Brown to follow suit and acquire Tickford.

When the Aston Martin DB2/4 MkII was introduced in 1955, Tickford produced the bodywork but final assembly was moved from Feltham all the way up to Meltham in Yorkshire – which is where David Brown tractors were manufactured. This was only a temporary arrangement, though. The DB MkIII came along in March 1957 and marked the point at which true Aston Martin production began at Newport Pagnell. Engines and bodywork would henceforth be made there, and assembly moved to the site from Meltham.

The family house that Joseph Salmons had built was demolished in 1963, but Sunnyside – long since converted into a single building – became Aston's head office and the original Salmons office block was retained. Although separated from Aston Martin Works by Tickford Street and no longer officially part of the Aston Martin Works site, they are protected as part of the town's conservation area – as is the 1910 workshop.

The Salmons & Sons works and (right) an aerial shot of the site after Aston Martin had taken over. Sunnyside is visible in the centre, while many of the factory buildings north of Tickford Street have since been replaced by housing. *AMHT*

Chapter 4

AN ICONIC DESIGN

ston Martin's relationship with renowned Italian coachbuilder Touring had started with the Federico Formenti-penned Superleggera Spyder. Based on a DB2/4 chassis, its low, sleek lines contrasted sharply with the traditionally upright standard car. Only three Superleggera Spyders would be built – chassis numbers AM300/1161, AM300/1162 and AM300/1163 – but they caused a sensation when they were displayed at the 1956 Turin, Paris and London motor shows.

When Aston Martin decided that its DB4 was to be designed by an Italian styling house, Touring was the natural choice. Harold Beach therefore travelled to Milan with the very early plans for the DB4's chassis, but Touring's response was that it needed to be a platform frame – rather than the perimeter style that Beach had envisaged – in order for its Superleggera system to be properly integrated. Beach returned to the UK and redesigned it in just six weeks.

The result was a robust steel structure that, in effect, comprised three sections: engine bay (including the bulkhead), cockpit (floorpans and sills – the transmission tunnel was glassfibre and non-structural) and boot (including rear suspension mounts). To this basic platform could be welded Touring's lightweight 'skeleton' of 5/8in steel tubes, which was used to support the aluminium body panels.

Formenti again took responsibility for the shape once this latest platform chassis was delivered to Touring, and what he came up with set the Aston template for the next 10 years. It was unmistakeably a product of that marque, but with an Italian flair and delicacy that won universal praise and made previous Aston designs look somewhat archaic. Unlike manufacturers such as Maserati and Alfa Romeo, which contracted Touring to build the cars as well as style them, Aston Martin instead took out a licence to use the Superleggera technique and construct the DB4 itself at Newport Pagnell.

There were many external tweaks throughout the course of its production run – the 1960 Series 2 replaced the Series 1's rear-hinged bonnet with a front-hinged panel, the Series 3 (April 1961) introduced the triple-light treatment for the rear, the Series 4 (September 1961) had a smaller bonnet air intake and the 1962 Series 5 had a longer body in order to increase interior space, plus the cowled headlights that had first been seen on the DB4 G.T.

In addition to its obviously reduced wheelbase – which necessitated a slightly different roof line – and those cowled lights, there were various other visual changes between DB4 and DB4 G.T. The bumpers were the same but minus their over-riders – they were eliminated completely on the Lightweight cars – and the door windows were frameless. As was to be

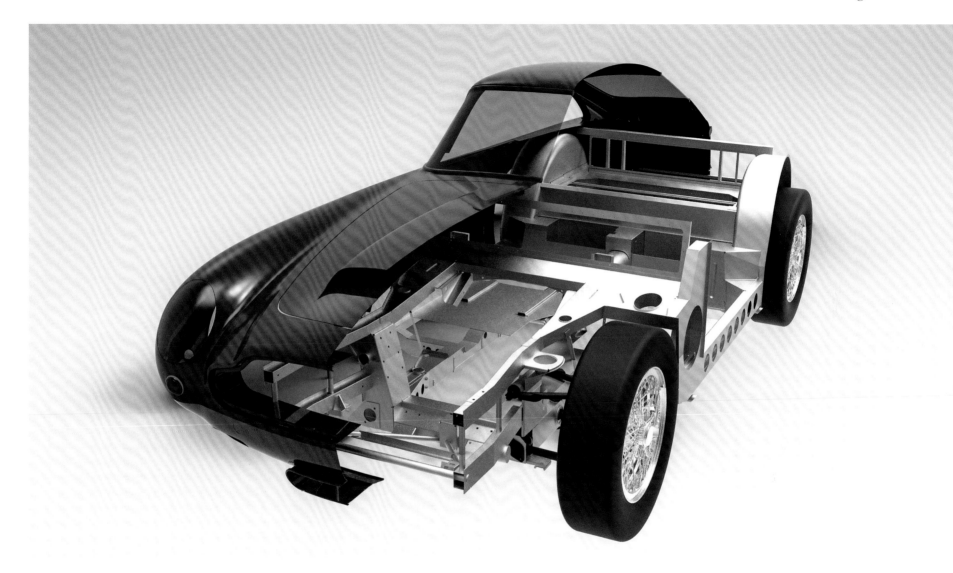

Detailed examination of period ◼
cars – including 3D scanning
– enabled the team to create
CAD renderings of the DB4 G.T.'s
structure and bodywork.

expected from a competition variant, the body weighed less – panels were made using 18-gauge magnesium-aluminium rather than 16-gauge – and in all the DB4 G.T. was 80kg lighter than its sibling. There were twin fuel-filler caps, too.

The G.T. also had the front-hinged bonnet from the start of its production run, while early cars had two small oil-cooler vents in place of the single larger duct that later G.T.s adopted. Other details, however, reflected the updates to the standard DB4. The bonnet-mounted air intake was one example, becoming more shallow on DB4 and DB4 G.T. alike from September 1961 onwards.

The hand-built and seemingly ever-changing nature of the

DB4 G.T. meant that restarting production from scratch threw up one particular challenge in terms of creating a styling template from which to work – each car was slightly different. The problem presented itself as soon as the team began to use the latest 3D laser-scanning techniques on a number of period G.T.s. Some of the original cars went to Newport Pagnell for the process to be carried out, but on other occasions the engineers instead went to the cars.

'Laser scanning is a non-destructive process that generates a collection of points in a 3D space,' explains Simon Hatfield. 'In effect, it's a huge game of 3D dot-to-dot that we connect to create a mesh. It's from this mesh that the surfaces can be

Superleggera construction laid bare – the basic platform structure is topped with a 'skeleton' of lightweight tubes that support the bodywork.

generated, and once we have that surface we can then use it in order to engineer the components and tooling, or to create a high-resolution render.'

The scanning proved that no two cars were exactly the same, and that the later ones were very different from the earlier models. Before they could finalise the spec of the continuation cars, the challenge was therefore to figure out what exactly their 'definitive' DB4 G.T. would be. As previously noted, the team concluded that it had to be to Lightweight specification, and it had to have the polycarbonate side and rear windows – only the windscreen is glass – plus the 'cathedral' style of tail-light cluster, as opposed to the later variant that had three individual lights. They also decided upon the original style of

headlamps – as worn by DP199 – which used exposed screws for the covers rather than the more refined aluminium rims that were used on later DB4 G.T.s.

'They are so hard to get looking nice,' says Hatfield with a smile, 'I understand why we moved to the aluminium-rimmed version!'

Once the specification had been decided upon and finalised, it was a case of sympathetically fine-tuning the shape to, for example, make it symmetrical – something that wasn't always the case with the period-built cars, but which surely would have been done had the technology existed. Now it does, so such refinements were a natural step.

'That actually caused us problems,' says Hatfield. 'We've

ended up with a symmetrical body, but the glass for the front windscreen wasn't quite symmetrical. We then had to rework the glass to make it symmetrical.

'We've had a few challenges. I'm a development engineer – I'm not a spreadsheet programme manager – and it's been nice for me to be able to do that level of engineering and work with my team to do that.

'We got [Aston Martin's] Gaydon studio involved to make sure that we got the curves correct and also to make sure that the car was what we wanted it to be – and that it looked like a DB4 G.T. It would have been very easy to give it to a styling house and they could have modified it to look like a modern car, but that's not what we wanted to do.

'We were quite strict in setting the guidelines as to what we wanted the car to look like. Some of our customers have got an original DB4 G.T. and they've got an original DB5. We want our car, our continuation DB4 G.T., to fit in that collection and for people not to be able to know the difference. It's been quite nice having our prototype parked next to an original car. Looking at the two together, you can say, "Yes – it looks like the car it's supposed to look like".'

Quite apart from getting the shape absolutely correct, there was a 60-year-old administrative matter to attend to.

'In period, there was an agreement with Touring of Milan for us to use their building technique,' explains Paul Spires. 'We've reinstigated that original contract with them. I went to

The famous flight case covered ■ thousands of miles and enabled owners to specify every aspect of their DB4 G.T. – from exterior colour to internal trim.

them and said, "We've got this agreement, wouldn't it be fun" – because commercially it makes no sense at all – "wouldn't it be fun to reinvoke that?" We're still building DB4s, so the agreement still stands…

'It's index-linked, but we're paying them exactly the same amount per body – I think it was £5 in period. We work closely with them and they've been really nice people to work with. They got really engaged with the car and they think it's great.'

With the DB4 G.T.'s exterior shape successfully captured via the scanning process, and Touring on board, the practical process of creating the body could begin.

'I was the engineering leader on one of the DB11 projects,' says Hatfield, 'so I knew some of the guys doing body on DB11, and the body was something that was so important to get right on the DB4 G.T. I stole one of those guys quite quickly…'

One of the most difficult aspects – and this is something that applied not just to the structure and the bodywork – was to balance quality requirements plus modern methods and materials with the authenticity that was at the forefront of Aston Martin's thinking.

'The customer expectation is very different now to 60 years ago,' confirms Hatfield. 'These are expensive cars and customers expect the same level of quality that they get from an expensive car now. We're never going to hit the levels of sealing and door-shut quality that we get on DB11 because that is the best-quality Aston Martin we've done so far. But where we are on DB4 G.T. is pretty damned good for a car that's, in effect, a re-engineered 1950s design. We're all immensely proud of what we've done and the product reflects that.

'There were some things that we could have gone away

■ For the continuation cars, the team settled on the earlier style of DB4 G.T headlamp, in which exposed screws are used to secure the Perspex covers. Later cars had an aluminium rim.

from. The windscreens, for example – we could have quite easily bonded those in and we'd have got infinitely better sealing, and that would have helped with things like wind noise. That's not what the car is, though. We've got to use the original way of building the car, which is aluminium panels over a steel chassis. We've not bonded parts together – we've fabricated and welded.

'We've still used jigging. There's not a single robot been employed in the manufacture of the chassis and the body. Yes, there are machined parts and pressed parts, and we've used the right technology where we've had to.'

The Newport Pagnell team worked with an external technical partner to produce the body panels, simply for reasons of time coupled with the desire for each of the 25 continuation bodies to be the same. A 'soft pressing' method was used, in which a pressurised rubber block presses an aluminium sheet over a soft tooled block to create the part.

The tooled block is epoxy, which is softer and quicker to machine than a traditional aluminium or steel tool but doesn't last as long – not a problem when you're making only 25 cars. The pressure and displacement of the rubber block can be tuned to minimise 'puckering' or splitting, and the whole process is repeatable and high-quality. In contrast, a 'hard pressing' normally needs two tools – a top section and a bottom section – in order to create a stamped part.

'Drawings, CAD and laser-cutting is all brilliant because it means that we increase the quality of the car,' continues Hatfield. 'Every part is the same. We've taken doors off one car and put them onto the next car. We've tried that to get that interchangeability throughout – it means that what we've done

All of the badges are as per the original, with the famous David Brown 'wings' logo even being remanufactured by the company that did it in period.

The interior has been painstakingly recreated, the only deviations from period cars being safety equipment such as the roll cage, harnesses and high-back seats.

is correct. If it fits the first car and fits the second car, it'll fit all the way to the 25th car.'

Key to the DB4 G.T.'s stance and overall look are the wire wheels – lightweight 5.5 x 16 centre-locks with triple-eared spinners and Dunlop L600 racing tyres.

'We could have quite easily gone to a wire-wheel manufacturer in the UK,' explains Hatfield, 'but the people who made the wheels are still operating in Italy. So, we've gone back to the original manufacturer – Borrani, which is a sister company to Touring. We've gone back through their archive as well and made sure that our thoughts on what we want to order match up with what's on their order book from back in the day.

They got all their old books out for us and we've gone back to that period spec exactly, which is really nice.'

That painstakingly thorough approach even went beyond the G.T.'s basic structure and major items such as wheels.

'The people that make the door latches – they haven't made them since the 1960s but it's the same company,' says Spires. 'They dusted off their tooling, found that it wasn't good enough, and retooled so that they could make our door locks.'

'The bonnet badges are still made by the same little shop in the jewellery quarter in Birmingham that made them originally,' adds Hatfield. 'Even down to the imperfections in how they're made. They're a glazed part – they're a piece of jewellery, really. They're enamelled, and they've got a lot of white in there and cream, and part of the enamelling process is that you sometimes get little black specks in the enamel. I got a lovely email explaining the process and they offered to go and spend some time in the enamelling shop.

'When we make the badges, they're bent – they're not flat. So we make them, then we send them off, get them bent and only then do we send them to get enamelled. We don't enamel it first and then get it bent because the enamel pops out.'

Before they started making the famous DB 'wings' badge, in fact, Spires had contacted Sir David's Brown widow, Paula, to get the family's permission. It was enthusiastically given.

The same attention to detail was also used for the car's interior. In period, the G.T.'s dashboard differed slightly from the standard DB4. Whereas the latter used readouts for amps and water temperature that were paired in a single gauge on one side, with those for oil pressure and fuel level arranged likewise on the other side, the G.T. had separate gauges for each one – as well as adding a fifth gauge for oil temperature. The rev counter, meanwhile, read to 7,000rpm rather than 'just' 6,000rpm. All of that would be faithfully reproduced on the continuation G.T.s, right down to the blue light filters on the sub-gauges and the G.T.-unique markings.

Other trim parts, such as switches and buttons, were still available but, as previously mentioned, often weren't considered to be of a good-enough standard, which led to Aston Martin having to retool where required – for the indicator stalks, for example. The engraving and paint-filling of switches was done especially for the continuation models to match the period style, and the 'LM' switch for the exterior Le Mans-style lighting is a unique touch.

When new, the DB4 G.T. was offered in 24 exterior colours, and there were 12 options for the interior. The Newport Pagnell team used the original records – as well as colour-scanning cars – to generate and perfect the colour pallet. As in period, Connelly leather has been used, that company's extensive records enabling it to tell Aston Martin which colours were ordered on a particular date.

The 'cathedral' tail lights have been adopted for each of the 25 continuation cars. In period, the DB4 G.T. featured both this style and the 'triple light' treatment.

To showcase all of this for the continuation cars, a flight case was created that contained samples and swatches of the available options. It ended up covering a lot of miles.

'We took that flight case around America to visit customers,' remembers Paul Spires with a smile. 'It was completely mad. Myself and a colleague flew in, went to New York, then rented a dreadful hire car and drove up to Boston. We spec'd another car there, drove back to New York and met with another customer, then flew to Chicago and met with another customer, then flew home from there. All in four days.

'There's a whole raft of stories of us doing things like speccing a car at 3 o'clock in the morning with a customer, in his kitchen and with the colours all over his worktop!'

The result of such effort and attention to detail is a car that does indeed blend into a line-up of period DB4 G.T.s. In that respect, it was mission accomplished in terms of the car's styling and interior.

'It would have been more profitable for us to make a pastiche,' explains Spires, 'to take a DB4 G.T.-looking body and put it onto a modern chassis, but that's not what this project is all about. It's as authentic as you can get in a modern car.'

■ Le Mans lighting has been recreated, while (left) Borrani was able to supply the wire wheels that it offered for the DB4 G.T. in the 1950s and '60s.

Touring of Milan

Touring of Milan was founded in 1926 by Felice Anderloni and Gaetano Ponzoni, who took over and renamed the Falco coachbuilding company. Anderloni was the stylist in the partnership, and the firm was soon producing bodywork for the likes of Isotta Fraschini and, in particular, Alfa Romeo – both of which were based nearby.

In its early days, Touring licensed Charles Weymann's method of constructing fabric bodies over lightweight tubing then, in 1937, it introduced its own system that employed small tubes to which aluminium panels were attached. The resulting structure was light and rigid, and Touring named the process Superleggera. The first car to use this innovative new design was Alfa Romeo's 6C-2300B.

Anderloni died in 1948, but his son Carlo took over alongside Federico Formenti. The years following WW2 would be Touring's golden era. It continued to work with Alfa Romeo – most notably, perhaps, on the spectacular series of Disco Volante models – and also created bodies for an eponymous new manufacturer that had been established in Maranello by Enzo Ferrari. In fact, Touring had previously been responsible for Enzo's Auto Avio Costruzioni 815 of 1940, before moving on to the beautiful little Ferrari 166MM as well as the subsequent 195, 212 and 340MM models.

Throughout the 1950s, its clients also included Pegaso, Maserati and Lancia, but Touring's business began to tail off in the 1960s as car firms increasingly started to style and produce bodywork in-house and switch to monocoque construction. Its relationship with Aston Martin, however, led to it styling the 1961 Lagonda Rapide, which borrowed heavily from the DB4 and shared that car's Superleggera construction.

Touring also built the bodies for the first production Lamborghini – the 350GT – and among its final styling projects was the Jensen Interceptor, but the renowned coachbuilder eventually closed its doors in 1966. Exactly 40 years later, it was revived when a new company bought the rights to the name. Fittingly, the current Carrozzeria Touring Superleggera is still based in Milan and still specialises in design and engineering.

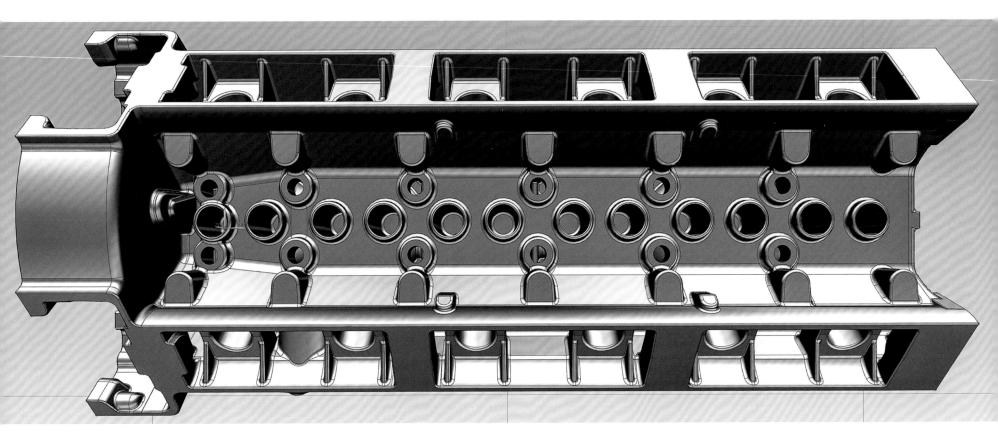

The heart of the DB4 was Tadek Marek's brand-new six-cylinder engine, for which the Polish engineer had been given responsibility as early as 1954. His initial plan was to use a cast-iron block, but this had to be revised for the very simple reason that the foundry Aston Martin wanted to use was already flat-out and didn't have the spare capacity. If it was to be an aluminium unit, however, one of its subsidiary businesses could get to work straight away.

Although he was initially sceptical – never having worked with aluminium before – Marek later conceded that it was the correct choice, although the production DB4 engine would suffer its fair share of teething problems.

Another change from his original brief was the eventual capacity of the 'six'. With one eye on racing regulations, it was thought that it should be a 3-litre unit but with the capability of being stretched for use in a new Lagonda model. Marek first began work on that larger variant, its 92mm x 92mm dimensions adding up to 3,670cc. It was ready for testing in late 1956 and, as it turned out, this would form the basic capacity of the DB4 unit, and be the starting point from which the engine would subsequently be enlarged for the DB5 and DB6. The 2,992cc variant never would see the light of day as a production unit, although one was built for use in the shortlived DBR3 of 1958. That same engine was fitted to the DB4 G.T. prototype,

DP199, for its ultimately unsuccessful 1959 Le Mans outing.

The new engine's twin overhead camshafts were driven off the crankshaft by Duplex chains, there were hemispherical combustion chambers, removable wet liners were used in the block and – in the standard DB4 – there was a single plug per cylinder and twin 2in SU HD8 carburettors on separate three-branch inlet manifolds. The crankshaft, meanwhile, was of nitrided steel and featured seven bearings. The powerplant was given the designation DP186 and produced a claimed 240bhp.

Maintaining Aston Martin's tradition of competition development, Marek's new engine was first used in the 1957 DBR2 sports-racer. That September, Roy Salvadori won at Silverstone and, in 1958, Stirling Moss won twice more – at Goodwood on 7 April and at Oulton Park the following week. Such results gave the powerplant a fine sporting pedigree by the time it was fitted into the DB4.

For the G.T. version of the engine, power was upped from 240bhp to 302bhp thanks to modifications such as twin plugs per cylinder – with twin distributors – triple twin-choke Weber DCO carburettors, high-lift camshafts and a compression ratio that was increased to 9:1. It was a lighter unit, too, due to the use of RR50 alloy in its construction.

There would be one more basic variant of Marek's powerplant used in the DB4, and in terms of specification it fell

■ The Newport Pagnell team produced a huge amount of CAD renderings for all areas of the DB4 G.T. – this is the twin-plug cylinder head.

roughly halfway between the standard DB4 and the G.T. It had triple carburettors, bigger valves and the G.T.'s 9:1 compression ratio, but Marek's goal was for it to remain tractable enough for comfortable road use. It produced 266bhp and would be fitted to the DB4 Vantage, which also gained G.T.-style cowled headlamps.

Restarting production of the G.T. engine in 2017 would involve more than the laser-scanning that was used for the car's exterior due to the obvious fact that the team also needed a complete internal blueprint. One way of achieving that would have been both expensive and sacrilegious – to cut up an original G.T. unit. With that clearly being out of the question, another solution had to be found.

'We went to the Nth degree on the engines,' says Hatfield, 'and ended up CT scanning them. It's effectively the same as an MRI scan – it sections an engine every 4-5mm so that you get an exact cut-through of it.'

If you mention CT scanning, you tend first to think of hospitals, but the process has a number of industrial and engineering uses. As well as the sort of reverse engineering that was key to the DB4 G.T. continuation project, it can help with quality control and failure analysis. X-ray measurements are taken from various angles in order to create an accurate cross-section image, and from that a CAD file can be generated. Not only did it enable the team to build up a blueprint for a DB4 G.T. engine without having to destroy an original, it enabled them to spot areas that could be improved – areas that, at the time, were limited by 1950s technology but which could benefit from the application of modern systems and processes.

'Working with our technical partners that we've got on DB11 at Gaydon,' explains Hatfield, 'we used the same people to help us redevelop [the DB4 G.T.'s] six-cylinder engine as we're using to manufacture the AE31 DB11 engine. That's a really nice thing to do, to use that same technology and bring the learning from DB11 to DB4 G.T.

'We actually got the chap who programme-managed the DB11 engine involved again. We had quite a few meetings down at Grainger & Worrall, which did the castings, and it was brilliant to see a man who understands how castings work and say, "Do you know what, we had this problem on DB9 or DB11 – let's fix it". We got the opportunity to make it right on our engine. That was great.'

There were other advantages that came from applying modern technology to the engine. In period, a number of

early DB4s suffered bearing failure due to the changes in their clearances when the engine got hot during extended high-speed running. As a result, period modifications included the addition of an oil cooler, increased sump capacity and adjusted clearances, and the engine was then extensively tested on the recently built M1 motorway by Bobby Dickson. In those days before speed limits, Dickson's best time for his regular 125-mile route was 56 minutes…

This trial-and-error system, necessary to a large extent because of the limitations of 1950s technology, could be bypassed on the continuation cars – the engines for which have been fine-tuned to 21st-century standards.

The engine block was the largest casting that was done for the continuation car. It matches the original (shown on the left) to the extent that it will drop straight into a period G.T.

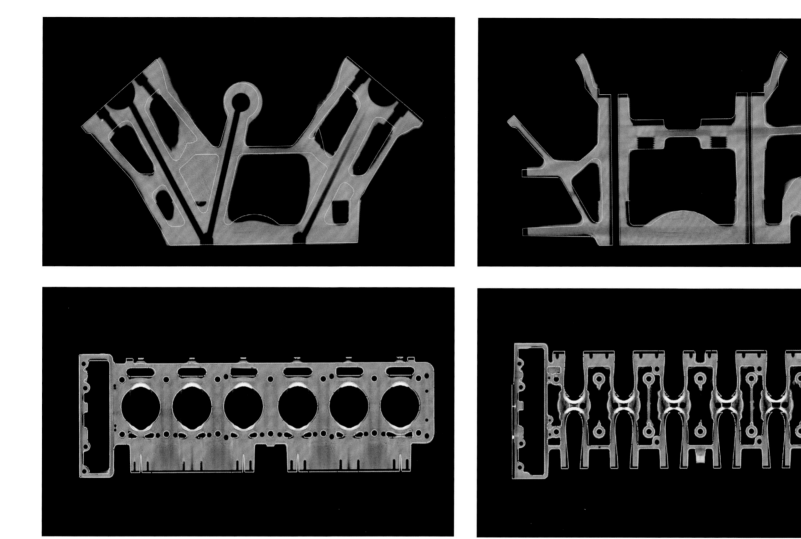

In order to get a complete internal view of the 'six', a CAT scan was carried out on an original engine. Better that than having to cut one up!

'We saw a huge number of anomalies within the [original G.T.] castings that told us that when they'd poured the molten metal in, certain bits of the mould shift and move,' explains Spires. 'Through CAE [computer-aided engineering] systems, we came up with a chilling process where all the crystals mesh together – whereas when you leave it to cool on its own, some of it meshes but as you go further out they actually clash so you get a very small instability.

'That's another reason why our engine delivers the power that it does and is lovely and smooth.'

Among the few changes to period DB4 G.T. specification was an increase in capacity to 4.2 litres, a standard upgrade to Marek's engine. Otherwise, the continuation powerplant remains faithful to the original but with the aforementioned advantage – as with the external elements such the bodywork – of modern analysis and manufacturing enabling Aston Martin to optimise the design.

'The materials are the same,' says Hatfield, 'and we were quite strict when we made the parts that they all had to be backwards-compatible. So, if we're making an engine block, I want that block to be able to go back into an original car. I also want an original engine, if they wanted to do this, to go into the continuation car. I wanted 100% compatibility on the engine, which we've got. We even put a 1959 engine into our first chassis, just to make sure that it could be done.

'The big thing for me was when we had an original block

plus the original drawings on the table, the CAD on a computer screen and the X-rays on a computer screen, and we had all this information around us. Do you know what? You could see the exact same features in all of these parts. That was the big moment with the engine.

'The block was the biggest casting that we'd done – the biggest part we've retooled and the most expensive part we've retooled. And to know that it's interchangeable and backwards-compatible is absolutely lovely. It's even down to little things like the core plugs and the castings – it's all in there.'

That ability to interchange parts meant that, for the sake of transparency, a 'C' was added to the continuation cars' engine number, which otherwise follows the same format as

the period DB4 G.T. And that's not the only detail that Hatfield and his team went to great lengths over.

'There's a really nice oil-cooler take-off on the engine block,' he explains. 'We'd seen a picture of a Le Mans engine in a book and thought, "We quite like that". Then we looked at the modern solution and thought, "We don't like that"!

'We went back and found a part, did the drawings, did the flow analysis, machined one from solid to make sure it fitted and would do what we wanted it to do, then got brave and got the company to make the castings.'

The standard DB4's gearbox was a four-speed all-synchromesh David Brown unit with a 10in Borg and Beck clutch. Although a 3.27:1 final-drive ratio had been specified

The standard production DB4 used a single-plug cylinder head, but that was upgraded to a twin-plug unit for the G.T.

for the prototype, Wyer felt that it was too high following his trans-European adventure-cum-test drive. The production car therefore had a 3.54:1 unit that gave 22mph per 1,000rpm in top, although there were also the options of 3.31:1 and 2.93:1.

The period DB4 G.T. came with the option of five rear-axle ratios, and a 9in twin-plate clutch replaced the 10in single-plate version. A close-ratio gearbox fed power to a Salisbury Powr-Lok limited-slip differential via an open propshaft. The continuation model features the same gearbox casing, which was retooled as per the original drawings, but with race-spec internals and no synchromesh – the dog 'box allows for much faster gearchanges on a car that, after all, will be driven hard on a track rather than more gently on the public road.

As for the suspension, when Harold Beach had originally started work on the DB2/4's intended replacement, he came up with a design that used wishbones and coil springs at the front, with a de Dion tube and trailing links at the rear. His very first prototype, DP114/2, wore Frank Feeley-penned bodywork and was eventually registered 4 MMC in August 1957 – it survives to this day – by which time development for the car that would become the DB4 had gone in a somewhat different direction.

The de Dion rear was dropped when it was discovered that the David Brown spiral bevel final drive – which was mounted

Left: the engine bay faithfully recreates that of period G.T.s – note the twin distributors driven off the rear of each camshaft. Right: vital to the 'feel' and stance of the G.T. is the use of Dunlop crossply tyres.

directly to the chassis – was far too noisy. Beach therefore switched to a Salisbury live axle with hypoid differential, and Touring then made up a further prototype – DP184/2 – using that layout. The Panhard rod set-up was replaced by a Watt linkage, and coils spring were used in conjunction with lever-arm dampers. At the front, the independent suspension comprised coil springs and wishbones with telescopic dampers – plus an anti-roll bar – while steering was via a David Brown rack and pinion system. Braking was by discs all round.

All of this was retained for the continuation G.T., but when the team was finalising the specifics of its set-up, the focus was on the fact that it will be used solely on a circuit.

'It's driven on special occasions,' explains Hatfield, 'and it's tuned for the track. It's not a road car, so you can get away with slightly stiffer suspension and a bigger anti-roll bar, plus firmer dampers. We used the prototype to tweak the geometry so that it behaves like a track car, and we've tuned it for a gentleman driver. We could have probably made it a little more aggressive but we didn't want it to be at the level where only Sir Stirling could jump in it and enjoy it! We want to give it to someone who might not have a lot of track-day experience.'

Left: triple Webers were fitted to the G.T. – the standard DB4 made do with a pair of SUs. Above right: even details such as the oil filler cap have been accurately recreated. Right: Watt linkage is clearly visible from underneath.

Despite the continuation car's track focus, engineers resisted the temptation to go overboard uprating the braking system. Solid discs are used, and there is no servo assistance.

'It's a mid-range car,' agrees Spires. 'It drives like an authentic 1959 G.T. It's not a full race car, nor is it a road car – it's right in the middle. It has the ability to go in either direction.

'What we want is to have a very high level of driver safety built into it because it's a quick car, make no mistake about that. We built the roll cage to FIA specification, the seats have got high backs with HANS devices, we've used six-point harnesses and we've got a fire-extinguisher system that sprays foam out of six different nozzles. We've gone up on safety from where they were originally.'

Among the few modifications is the use of Rose joints rather than rubber bushes, which was done purely for reasons of durability. The springs and dampers are also slightly stiffer, but not to any great degree – the requirement was for it to still drive like a 1959 DB4 G.T. 'It doesn't feel like a current FIA-spec car,' confirms Spires. 'It's nowhere near as low or as stiff as those. And that why it looks right.'

Another reason is that the continuation G.T. uses the original specification of crossply tyres.

'That delivers the main handling feel of the car,' explains Hatfield. 'The tyres are the bit that touch the ground. Yes, you've got bum to seat, seat to floor, floor to suspension, suspension to tyre, tyre to ground. But the big one is tyre to ground – that's what makes the car feel the way it does. And by sticking to the original crossply tyres, we've kept that feel.

'It's a nice thing to do, and it shows that, as a company, we respect our history. We could have quite easily put a modern engine into an old chassis and made it infinitely quicker than it is. OK – it's still got 350bhp. It's not a slow car! We could have put injection on it, we could have given it a modern gearbox, we could have done all of those things. But we haven't. We could have put servo brakes on it, but we haven't. We've not put silly discs on it. We've gone for a nice, progressive set-up that a gentleman driver can get straight into.'

Tadek Marek

■ Marek (pictured centre) was a key figure during the David Brown era, and masterminded the DB4's six-cylinder powerplant. *AMHT*

Now inextricably linked to Aston Martin, Marek was born in Krakow in 1908 and studied engineering at Berlin's Charlottenburg Technical Institute. Despite a much later, and seemingly erroneous, quote from Aston Martin's Ted Cutting that suggested Marek didn't much like motor racing, the Pole developed an interest in competition on both two wheels and four. In 1928, however, he suffered a big accident that resulted in the loss of a kidney as well as hundreds of soda syphons that were in the marquee that he hit.

Marek subsequently returned to his homeland to work for Fiat and General Motors, but nonetheless he continued to compete in major events. He entered the Monte Carlo Rally three times during the late 1930s – in 1937, he drove a Fiat 1100, in 1938 a Lancia Aprilia and 1939 an Opel Olympia. He even won the 1939 Poland Rally at the wheel of a Chevrolet.

During the war, Marek joined the Polish Army but in 1941 travelled to the UK, where his engineering talents were put to good use working on the Rolls-Royce Meteor engine that was fitted to Centurion tanks. When hostilities ended, he briefly moved to Germany to assist with relief efforts as part of the United Nations Relief and Rehabilitation Association, but was back in England by 1949. Following two years of being unemployed, he joined Austin at Longbridge.

Marek moved to Aston Martin in early 1954 after a recruitment process that was complicating by his mistakenly receiving a letter saying that his services wouldn't be required after all. As well as the DB4's six-cylinder engine – story has it that he fitted his personal DB4 road car with a 4-litre Vantage-spec unit – he would go on to be responsible for the V8 that was first fitted to the DBS in 1969. That was two years after the radical new Williams Towns-designed model had been introduced with Marek's trusty 'six'; by the time that the V8 made it into the production car, Marek had left the UK and moved to Italy. He subsequently returned and died in the Hampshire village of Selborne in 1982.

Chapter 6
ENGINEERED TO PERFECTION

Two prototypes were used for the initial phase of the DB4 G.T.'s development programme. PP0 was what Paul Spires refers to as a 'laboratory car' and enabled the team to work on components such as the electrical system, engine installation and suchlike. It was never built up into a complete car – it was merely a rolling structure on which the fitment of major components could be tested.

In the meantime, PP1 was used to perfect the bodywork and the structure itself, the existence of the two prototypes enabling more progress to be made in a short space of time. Once it was ready, everything from PP0 was transferred on to PP1 and development continued on the latter car alone. Fittingly, PP1 was finished in the same Ecurie Trois Chevrons colour scheme as DP199 had been back in 1959.

The deadline for having PP1 ready was late September 2017, which was when it was due to be delivered to the south of France so that it could take part in filming for an episode of *The Grand Tour*. The Build Centre team worked around the clock to make it happen, Simon Hatfield signing off a time sheet for 97 hours per week for one of the technicians in the run-up to handing it over to Jeremy Clarkson and co.

On Friday 15 September, the prototype was fired up, rolled out of the Build Centre and driven down the workshop. To honour the occasion, the Newport Pagnell factory had closed 10 minutes early so that everyone could come and watch. Hatfield recalls the satisfaction in having those few people who'd predicted how much they'd struggle to complete the project coming up and offering their congratulations and enthusiastic praise.

The following day, work continued into the night. In order to be able to use the car on the public road, PP1 had been registered as a prototype, which meant that it could follow in the wheeltracks of DB4s that had left the factory nearly 60 years previously.

'The car was finished at about 11pm,' recalls Spires with a smile. 'Simon jumped into the passenger seat, I jumped into the driver's seat, and we drove Newport Pagnell's first new car in 10 years up Tickford Street at 11.30pm. It was dark and it was drizzly and it was foggy, but that was a moment in history. And the car worked!'

As you'd expect, Hatfield also has a very clear memory of the moment, describing the first drive 'with a very excited Paul, and a nervous me in the passenger seat…'

They turned off the lights at Aston Martin Works at 1am that night, and were back at 6am on Sunday 17 September so that PP1 could be driven – not transported, driven – to the nearby Millbrook Proving Ground for its shakedown tests. Even at a venue such as Millbrook, where exotic machinery is hardly a

Testing of PP1 gets under way at Millbrook Proving Ground. The car was driven there from Newport Pagnell.

rarity, the DB4 G.T. was without doubt the star attraction.

'Other people from within the industry were there,' remembers Hatfield, 'all the different supercars were [being] tested, but for those couple of days we were the most interesting thing there. Everyone wanted to talk about the car – it's created a buzz within the industry.

'It would be lovely if it had been instantly perfect, but that's the point of having a development car – we always knew that we'd find things to develop and things that we needed to make better. That said, we did two days of shakedown and didn't have a single mechanical problem, then it went off and did 1,000 miles with a film crew, wheel-spinning, donuts – you name it. I think that's testament to the level of the car.'

The Millbrook 'running in' was carried out by Aston Martin's

lead Performance Driving instructor Simon Dickinson, who impressed the team so much that he soon became the Chief Test Driver and would eventually go on to complete PP1's dynamic sign-off.

From Millbrook, PP1 went straight to the south of France so that it could take part in filming for *The Grand Tour*. Ben Amos was the engineer who accompanied it.

'On a typical day we'd be up early because they would want the cars ready to go at 8.30am,' he recalls. 'We would have gone over everything the night before, so we'd just give the car a quick check to ensure everything was still as it should be.

'Then we'd head to the first filming location of the day, which was usually not too far from where we were staying. We had a Transit van that had a fairly large variety of tools and spares and

The team fettles PP1 ahead of its maiden test, including putting protective film around the vulnerable front end.

was never too far from the car. Again, on arrival we'd check over the basics – making sure the wheel spinners were still tight, that sort of thing.

'Then filming would begin. The crew wanted us to be on hand should they have any issues or if they wanted to add or remove bits – the copper-cored HT leads give off a lot of electrical interference so they were constantly trying to work around that with their equipment.'

With the fierce temperatures that were encountered during some of the filming – particularly while they were in Pau – the Aston Martin team was also there to provide a bottle of water and a towel at the end of each run! At one point, Jeremy Clarkson drilled two 'air conditioning' holes into PP1's fixed Perspex driver's window. The offending panel got changed when the car returned to Newport Pagnell, and soon afterwards PP1 gained working window mechanisms, which negated the need for such extreme measures.

'At around midday the filming would halt for an hour for lunch,' continues Amos. 'That allowed us a bit of time to act on anything that had been reported back to us. After lunch, it would likely be on to the next location. It might have been a fair drive so the "star cars" would drive in convoy up ahead with crew and support vehicles – including our van – in convoy a little way behind. On arrival at the location, we'd once again have a check over the car and give it a wipe down, then we'd be on hand again during the filming.

'Once that had been completed for the day it would be on to the next hotel – typically an hour or so driving, arriving at about 7pm. We would then get more of a chance to give the car

Joe Waters climbs on board at Millbrook. PP1 proved to be remarkably reliable straight out of the box, including its trip to the South of France for *The Grand Tour* and to Nardò for further testing.

Simon Dickinson (in the driving
seat) and Paul Spires prepare
to take the car out during the
Millbrook tests.

a full inspection – checking all of the fluids, taking the wheels off to check for wear, ensuring all suspension fixings were all tight, etc. Depending on what we found, that could take until 8.30-9pm, then we'd have an evening meal with the crew and go to bed, ready to do it all again the next day!'

Remarkably, over the course of 968 miles, and lots of repeat runs for the camera, PP1 performed with aplomb: 'Mostly it was just monitoring everything because the car had not long been built and had only minimal testing, so we were keen to keep an eye on every aspect. Fortunately, it was very well behaved. It ran out of fuel, which only happened the once because we had a problem with the fuel sender so the gauge was mis-reading. And we lost reverse gear, something that happened during the day's filming but which we had to wait until the evening to

have a look at. It turned out to be a matter of just adjusting the clutch travel.

'Driving conditions varied greatly, too. There was town driving in Pau – the car didn't enjoy that too much because the outside temperature was very hot and it involved a lot of slow driving in traffic but nonetheless it did very well. There was a fair amount of cruising on the French and Spanish highways, then up and down the Pyrenees.

'We were interested to see what the altitude did to the car's running temperature because this is something we've encountered before on classic Astons, but the temperatures were exactly where we would like to see them.

'The whole experience was fantastic. The car was very well received by the crew and Clarkson, Richard Hammond and

Millbrook's vast facilities
allowed for testing to be carried
out on its high-speed bowl (left)
as well as its challenging
Alpine-esque Hill Route (above).

The intention was to give the continuation car the feel of the original G.T. rather than lowering it and stiffening it too much, which would have robbed it of that period-style character.

James May. They were all impressed with its performance and durability, and with how quickly the car had been built and to such a high standard.'

On its return from filming, PP1 went back to its exhaustive testing schedule at venues around the UK. It first went to Snetterton, where its dynamic assessment was carried out, along with fine-tuning of the springs and dampers. Matt Becker – Aston Martin's Chief Engineer Vehicle Engineering – drove it during this period, as did Ray and Michael Mallock. Ray Mallock's presence offered a nice piece of continuity because during the 1980s he'd been involved with both the Aston Martin-engined Nimrod Group C car – which he raced for marque stalwart Viscount Downe

– and then the thunderous Aston Martin AMR-1.

The roads around Newport Pagnell were used for general fault-finding, but PP1 was also taken as far afield as the Nardò proving ground in southern Italy. There, Aston Martin Racing's Darren Turner – twice a class winner at Le Mans in the DBR9 – was joined by former AMR team-mate Peter Dumbreck and Wolfgang Schuhbauer. As Director of Aston Martin's Nürburgring Test Centre, Schuhbauer heads a team of 12 engineers that carry out 8,000km of final testing on every new model at the famous German circuit.

Each member of the trio was therefore familiar with endurance testing, which came in very useful as PP1 racked up 2,500km around Nardò. Again, there were no problems at

all, Hatfield recalling that the car 'amazed us all – we just kept feeding it fuel and tyres…'

'None of them managed to break it!' says Spires of the drivers who took part in testing. 'The bits that we had to do on the car were minute – they were small things. But in probably 4,000 miles of driving, it's never broken down. It's never failed to start. Darren Turner did one hour 46 minutes in one stint – we have got the most incredibly robust car and that was straight out of the box.'

Silverstone was also used for fine-tuning of the carburettor set-up and, in January 2018, a number of media test-drives. In fact, PP1 doubled as a press car throughout its testing schedule – after its adventure on *The Grand Tour*, it went to Goodwood on 2 October 2017 for a photoshoot with *Octane* magazine – and in that way it echoed the use of DP199 in period.

After being registered 845 XMV, DP199 was the car in which Reg Parnell set a best time of 20 seconds for going from 0-100mph-0. It was also road-tested for *Car and Driver* by Dennis May. Following its time as a development and test car, it was sold in June 1961 to the Honourable Gerald Lascelles – cousin to Queen Elizabeth II – and subsequently owned by the likes of Mike Salmon and marque enthusiast Rowan Atkinson. It survives to this day, and was sold at auction in 2017 for $6,765,000. In fact, the parallels with the continuation project don't end there – once it had completed its test programme and media commitments in early 2018, PP1 was also sold, and left Newport Pagnell for a new life in America.

Considering that the DB4 G.T. had first appeared in 1959, road-tests of it were rather slow in appearing. In the December 1961 issue of *Motor Racing* magazine, however, Jack Fairman – a man with immense experience of racing Aston Martins – wrote a thorough track-test and relished driving 'something with bags of power under my right foot and a built-in feeling of solidity or even indestructability.'

'I would rate the car as extremely well balanced,' he continued, 'and I can honestly say that in all the hundreds of miles I have driven the DB4 G.T., not once has it spun me off the track… and I haven't exactly been hanging about at times!'

Fairman noted the Aston's slight tendency towards understeer, but said that: 'This, I think, suits the car well, because there is ample power available to flick the tail out should you want to do so.'

He concluded thus: '…for the private owner, who likes to drive hard and indulge in some pretty effective GT racing on his

own account, I'm sure that he will find in the Aston I've been writing about a car that will be man enough for the job and a delightful possession to boot.'

That same month, 0167 – a Lightweight model registered 40 MT and also used by the factory for development work – was tested by John Bolster for the 8 December issue of *Autosport*. Bolster was an extremely experienced racer and test-driver, noting of the DB4 G.T. that: '…this Grand Touring car is considerably faster than the single-seaters that I used to drive in Grand Prix races not so many years ago!'

As with Fairman, Bolster revelled in the Aston Martin's balance – 'One may encompass extreme angles of drift without any fear of dropping it' – as well as its high-speed stability and its engine, which he wrote 'makes all the right noises and

The lack of modern driving aids means that the DB4 G.T. is a very 'human' car to drive. Its set-up had been optimised by the likes of Aston racer Darren Turner.

seems to be enjoying itself.' He signed off by calling the DB4GT a 'stupendous high-performance car' that 'looks the thoroughbred that it is, and must be placed high on the list of the world's most desirable touring cars.'

That was the high standard against which PP1 would be measured and which had to be in the minds of everyone who was involved with the testing and development – as was making it feel like a 1959 car rather than a 2018 one.

'It's been very interesting to get different drivers from different backgrounds to drive it,' explains Spires. 'Everybody's loved it – no matter where they've come from. I've said to the professional racing drivers, "I know what you're going to say, you're going to say that it's too soft. You boys always say that everything's too soft. Just drive it as you would a 1959 car and then you'll get into it."

'They have fun with it because it dances around, the tail moves. You feel the car on its tip-toes – almost like a ballerina. You're in complete control – there's nothing electronic about it. You can just go and enjoy it.

'Someone who's driven a 1959 car and PP1 should be able to say, "That's the same car". A lot of these guys haven't driven a DBGT, so they get out and say, "Is this how they were?" Yep! But then the more they get it into it, the more they understand it and the more they get it.'

'It is definitely very rewarding to drive,' agrees Hatfield. 'If you tell the car what you want it to do, it will do it. If you put that sequence of bends together and you've got the downshifts right, and you've been progressive on the brakes, the smile you get is great. There's no ABS, there's no traction control, there's no ESP, no active differential, no active suspension, no servo on the brakes even – it is a mechanical car.

'And it's a beauty to behold. When you get all of those things right, the smile it gives you is unlike the smile that you'll get from a modern car.'

Spires: 'If you jump out of something modern, with traction control and ABS and big fat tyres and aerodynamic devices, then jump into this – with spindly crossply tyres and no aerodynamic devices – and you're driving it on the throttle and it's got a dog gearbox as well, it'll be quite an experience. I'm convinced that people will be blown away by it.

'I liken the car to a Spitfire. This is a car where, if you drive it beautifully, it'll feel beautiful, and it'll tell you whether you're driving it well or you're driving it badly. There's a human interaction with it. You become at one with it and it becomes personal to you. You feel a connection and there's a definite reward, which you might not get with modern cars – however fast they are and however good they are. It's a lovely thing – just the most superb car to drive.'

With all of the initial planning and engineering for the DB4 G.T. continuation cars having been done in Newport Pagnell, and with PP0 and PP1 having been built there and tested there, it was time for the 25 customer cars to go into production. As soon as the team had received the green light at the very beginning of the project, a bespoke Build Centre had been created within the Service Department that had room for three cars to comfortably be assembled side by side.

'I don't think you could build this car anywhere else,' says Paul Spires. 'This is its spiritual home – it has to be built in Newport Pagnell because of the provenance. DB4 G.T.s were built here 60 years ago; they're being built here again. When the last car was finished in 2007, it was a pretty dismal day – for Aston Martin and for Newport Pagnell. This whole town has grown up with Aston Martin being a phenomenal part of it. Not just Aston Martin but Salmons and Sons, and Tickford Coachworks. This site predates the internal combustion engine.

'This place came very close to closing when production finished. It would have been very easy for everybody to say, "Newport Pagnell is finished – we've moved to a new location", as we did when we shut down Bloxham and everything moved to Gaydon. It would have been very easy for this place not to exist, but fortunately it does. There's some really key skills

around the area. When you go up into the town centre with an Aston Martin Works jacket on, people come up to you and say, "It's wonderful to hear that production is restarting and isn't it great that the business is thriving?" That amount of local support can't be underestimated.

'Even without the DB4 G.T., Works was thriving and expanding. But I think that, for people who've worked here a long time, to see that we're building cars again – the whole company has a dynamic feel about it, that we can go and do these cars. This is a very sophisticated, well-oiled, well-run part of the business, and there's a lot of people working on this programme – it isn't a couple of guys at Newport Pagnell sitting in the corner building cars.

'[Aston Martin CEO] Andy Palmer said that, in the same year that we launched Valkyrie, we launched DB4 G.T. – there's no other car company in the world that has done that, that has looked at both ends of the spectrum and taken those on. I think that Andy's very brave and he's a visionary when it comes to that kind of stuff, to allow us to do those sorts of projects.'

All of the DB4 G.T. assembly is done in the Build Centre by a team of technicians, overseen by a quality engineer, a build engineer and two project engineers.

'There are different ways of making a car go together,' says Simon Hatfield, 'and we've got to do a mix of the old and

■ Once the continuation project was confirmed, a new Build Centre was constructed in the Works Service department.

the new. If we used every single new method under the sun to make it, it would look like a new car. It wouldn't look like a continuation car. There is the hand-crafting in there – the tickling, the fettling – but at the same time we've used the methods that we know from making new cars. So, new ways of making the quality of the car better. We can make nicer extrusions for the rubbers and the seals, for example, and they make a big impact on how the cars actually go together.

'The car's fully in CAD, which I don't think has been done for a DB4 or any other Heritage car that we have. That really helped all the way through, from different function checks to why Part A doesn't match Part B. Technicians can go back and say, "The engineers say it should and the designer says they should, but the two parts don't marry up". It's a lovely way of understanding what's wrong – it's the definitive way, because you've got a measurement on one piece of CAD that's made from an original drawing and you've got a physical part in your hand. You can put the two together with the drawing on your desk and you can compare all three and actually figure out what's wrong.

'Sometimes, we've found a few errors in the drawings, which might be down to the fact that we've got an earlier drawing and

■ Despite the adoption of modern techniques for some areas of the car, there's still a lot of fettling and hand-finishing that needs to be done. Templates (left) are used in order to correctly position holes for fixtures and fittings.

A 'pre-fit' procedure is carried ■ out in the Build Centre before the cars goes to the paint shop. Rather than having major components, such as the engine, sitting around waiting for a chassis, they're ordered using a 'just in time' system.

it was up-issued – or we've only got the up-issued one and not the original. Having it all in CAD is very useful for understanding and trying to make sure that we don't get these clashes. And adjustability, too. Before, things used to be adjusted by hand – heated up, bent a little bit and put in. We've now gone to the level of building in the tolerance and the float.

'It's great to bring back some of the techniques from DB11 to DB4 G.T. – our newest car going back to help the oldest. It's lovely when people from Gaydon come over to talk to us about what we're doing on DB4. We bring up a document and they instantly recognise it because it's a document that they use at Gaydon. And the engineers and managers are used to seeing the format. It helps them understand that we're doing it properly. We're not just four blokes in a shed, bashing cars together. We're doing it properly.

'We've been lucky in that, having the experience of doing all the restorations here, we could quite easily go to one of the [Heritage Centre] lads and say, "We're having a bit of a problem – where do you get these bits from?" Or, "Have you any experience in how this bit goes together?" We've got so much knowledge here. We've got a small machine shop on-site.

■ Fitting the famous Superleggera badge (top left) and (left) prepping the boot lid. Three of its sides are trimmed by hand in order to fit the aperture.

I once needed some bits turning down at the end of the day when everyone was about to go home, and I shouted down, "You haven't got 20 minutes to turn these down, have you? I need them before the weekend." Fifteen minutes later they were done. And you think, "Yeah – everyone wants this to come together". I'd often get a nudge on a Thursday with people asking if we needed a bit of extra help over the weekend. People just helping out.'

The cars are built at the rate of two per month. External technical partners supply the engines, chassis and panels to the specifications that have been meticulously laid down by the Newport Pagnell engineers, who continue to work closely with them throughout the production run.

'We're working with people who can move as quickly as we can,' explains Hatfield of the supply chain. 'We're a small team, with a great supplier base behind us who have helped us every single step of the way.'

'It's very much as it was back in the day,' says Spires. 'Parts come in, and we'll fit bodies to chassis here, put the driveline in, plumb it, wire it, paint it, trim it. This car has probably got the highest content of UK-manufactured parts of any car that's

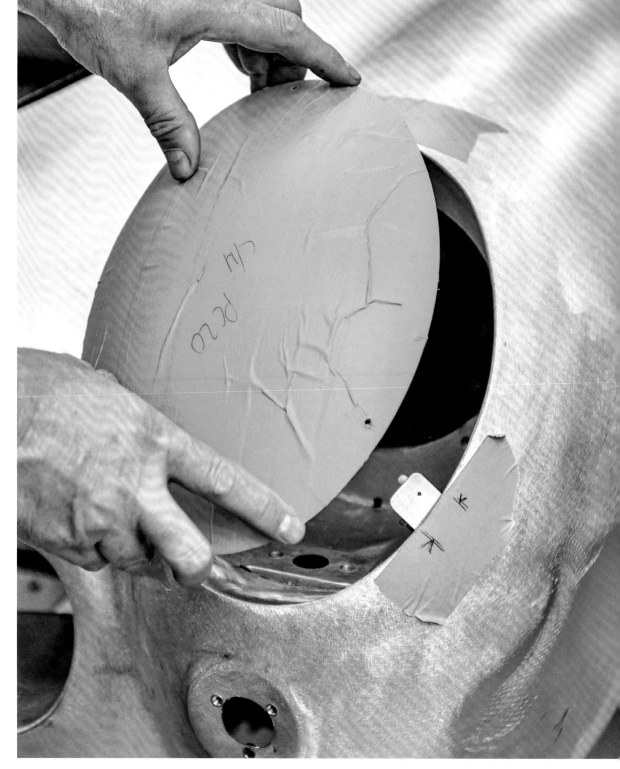

Fitting the Perspex covers to the headlamps – their use on the DB4 G.T. in period provided a preview of the updated styling that would subsequently be adopted on the DB5.

built in the UK. We make the bodies here, the chassis here, the engines here, the gearbox, the back axle. The wheels come from Italy, but other than that it's very, very high in UK content.

'With the UK car industry, we're very adept at making a small number of components very quickly. Because we're in "motorsport valley" here, there are a lot of people that we can draw on. It wasn't easy, but the skill levels are there and the companies exist that you can go to and say, "Make me 32 of these little widgets" and they'll bang them out in a couple of weeks. So we were able to tap into that, which you don't necessarily get in other parts of the world.'

While acknowledging the support of external companies throughout the project, the key engineering and technical expertise had to be focused upon Newport Pagnell.

'The core skills are here,' says Spires. 'We've taken some people from the modern service side who again have come into the Build Centre and they've learnt on DB4 G.T. some of the older skills that might have been forgotten.

'I always think that the modern side of the business is fantastic, but with a lot of it the computer tells you what's wrong with the car, and you take one bit off and put another unit on. That's massively over-simplifying it, but it's quite nice for some of these guys to get back to core skills.'

As the build programme got under way, the ripple effect could be felt throughout Aston Martin. 'There's definitely been a boost,' says Spires. 'A lot of people have been engaged – even people who were sceptical when I first announced that we were going to do this car have come on board and realised that actually, this thing is real. It's happening.'

'It's special,' agrees Hatfield. 'I get a couple of emails a week from someone in the company saying that they'd seen a picture

■ Richard Neill is a Newport Pagnell veteran, and it's his job to ensure that all of the panels fit correctly before each car goes down to the Build Centre.

of it and that it looks cool, or they're driving past Newport Pagnell next week and want to pop in to have a look. We say yes, as long as they bring something nice from Gaydon! So they bring a test car and we can have a bit of a natter about the whole thing.

'It's not robots doing this,' he concludes. 'It's not just people who are there to clock in and clock out every day. They're fully invested in it.'

One of those who is most definitely invested in it is Dave Alderman, a coachbuilder by trade who joined Aston Martin in 1990. His career at Newport Pagnell coincided with the last of the V8s and setting up of the Virage line, and he also worked on the Lagonda as that model trickled through towards the end of its production life. He was soon promoted to end-of-line rectification for the Virage, handling the final sign-off procedure.

'Then Vanquish came on board,' he recalls, 'which was completely different. All of a sudden, we went from having one or two engineers to engineers being everywhere, and it was a massive explosion in terms of electronics and suchlike. I was process leader for end-of-line on Vanquish. Every car was road-tested at Millbrook – it was great fun.'

Alderman admits that ending production at Newport Pagnell in 2007 'broke our hearts'. The majority of the site had been

Dave Alderman joined Aston Martin in 1990 and boasts a wealth of production experience. Here he fits the trim around the rear window.

■ Completing the engine bay on PP1. Having the car fully rendered in CAD made life easier in terms of ensuring that parts would fit first time.

based on land to the north of Tickford Street – now largely being redeveloped for housing – while Works Service and the present-day facility lay to the south of it. Talk to any Newport Pagnell veteran and it won't take long for them to refer to working 'over the road'. With the Vanquish run coming to an end, Alderman crossed Tickford Street and started to work on the restoration of Aston Martin's classic models.

'It was an eye-opener for me when I first came over to work on restorations. It took me six months to get used to slotted-head screws and all that sort of thing. It's just a different world – 2BA, 4BA, 5/16s UNF – all that sort of thing. But I knew it inside-out when I moved to DB4 G.T.

'I was a technician, so I'd strip all the cars down – and I still specialised in the body side of things. I did DB2/4s, MkIIIs, DB4s, 5s and 6s, Volantes – I did a lot of work on Prince Charles's car. Then, when Paul Spires first said about the DB4 G.T. continuation project, I said to him, "This is right up my street". I had 20 years in production and it's built into me to make

something better every time we do it, make it neater. I'd also restored a lot of DB4s and G.T.s, so I knew the car.'

One of the major advantages of the DB4 G.T. continuation project was opportunity to bring together experienced hands such as Alderman with younger guys such as Joe Waters, who joined Aston Martin as an apprentice in 2005 and has always worked at Newport Pagnell.

'When I first started I was in the main workshop,' says Waters, 'when the Heritage cars and modern cars were all in the same area. I was mainly doing general servicing, but then Heritage was separated and I stayed on the modern side. I gained a lot of experience with special projects, doing track days with One-77s and V12 Zagatos – fitting telemetry into them, that sort of thing. With the DB4 G.T. being a track car and very much a special project, it was obviously interesting to me.'

As technicians, Alderman and Waters are perfectly placed to explain the build process. When a powder-coated chassis arrives at Newport Pagnell, the first job is to inspect it and

Modern techniques have ■ ensured that the continuation car features much more efficient seals than the DB4 G.T. would have had in the 1950s and '60s.

seam-seal it, then rivet in the lightweight floorpans and bulkhead panels, before the exterior body panels can be fitted.

'There's a lot of work involved in finishing the panels off before fitting them to the car,' says Alderman. 'That's done by our panel shop. It's as skilled as it's ever been. They're forever fettling and cutting and welding – it's not just a simple process where you bolt it on.'

Richard Neill is one of those to whom this process is entrusted. He's been with Aston Martin for 33 years, from V8 and Virage all the way to Gaydon, before being 'borrowed' for the DB4 G.T. continuation project.

'We have to wire the edges where required,' he explains, 'which means curving them round some steel wire to give it strength and ensure that it keeps its shape.

'There's a lot of work involved in finishing the panels off before fitting them – it's as skilled as it's ever been'

Fitting the interior: the roll cage, which is standard fitment for the continuation car, is removed in order to improve access during this stage of the build.

Joe Waters working on the interior: he started as an apprentice at Newport Pagnell and has moved across to the continuation project from modern Aston Martins.

'We trial-fit all of the panels here. The doors come in done, so in theory we shouldn't have to do anything to those beyond turning the edges [folding the outer panel over the inner]. The boot is ready-turned along its upper edge, but then we grind in the other three edges. The bonnets come in with the rear edge turned but we have to grind the rest of it in.'

'Everyone's scared of closing a bonnet once the engine's in!' says Alderman. 'You've got the little post that goes into the lock – if you get that slightly off-centre, it'll wedge itself in and you can't open it again! It's important to get that right.'

'It's critical what they do here,' he adds of the panel shop, 'because when we fit them we can't be coming back saying, "This isn't right – this panel's too big". Although, it's hand-made so you do get discrepancies.'

When the panel shop has finished with the car, it gets rolled the 100 metres or so down to the Build Centre on dollies and the team then carries out what Alderman describes as 'pre-fit'. Part of that process is drilling the necessary holes. Neatly arranged in a drawer is a set of templates that are used to

ensure that the holes go in exactly the correct place for fixtures such as the windscreen wipers – for both left- and right-hand-drive cars – the rear lights, the badges, and the chrome surround for the boot lid.

The inlet for the oil cooler gets fabricated and the grille made up – the latter has to be bespoke to each car simply because the hand-finished nature of the aperture means that each one is slightly different. The door internals are added and the technicians also ensure that the opening panels, once fitted, latch correctly. In the very earliest days of the project, they had to consider such details as the car's use of imperial fittings, and making sure that they had the correct tools for those. The only metric fittings you'll find on a continuation DB4 G.T. will generally be in the modern safety systems – the seats, harnesses, fire extinguisher and roll cage.

'In certain ways, it's easier than putting together a period DB4 G.T.,' says Waters, 'because everything's clean and brand new. An original car might have been taken apart and put back together a few times. But there are still parts that, if they're at one end of the tolerance and you're at the other end, won't quite meet in the middle. With the body side, we get the raw panels and everything needs to be fettled – it's the same with the rest of the car. We get the parts in, but everything just needs a slight touch to make it perfect.'

With the engine bay remaining in its powder-coated finish, the straight-six can be fitted before the car gets sent to the paint shop. The suspension can also go on at this stage.

'When we get the car back from paint,' says Alderman, 'one of the first jobs is to get the headlining in. Before that, though, the wooden cant rails that go down the sides are only roughly made so we need to trim them to size. Where wood goes around the rear wheelarches, that all has to be individually fitted, too – no two are the same. After that's all trimmed, the wiring loom can go in.'

All of the trim is produced and fitted at Newport Pagnell, and those cant rails are far from being the only things that have to be fettled on each car. The stainless-steel B-post finishers, for example, have to match the rear edge of the door glass, so they can only be made once the door is in and they know the angle of the glass.

One of the last things to be fitted is the bolt-in roll cage – the chassis arrives with it in place, but obviously the team has to immediately remove it for reasons of access – followed by the seats. The latter are modern high-backed units, but could be replaced by period ones if required. Likewise, the roll cage can be removed completely, leaving you with an interior that even more closely matches that of an original DB4G.T.

'We pre-fitted everything [on the prototype] and we had a big board where we noted everything that was wrong,' says Alderman. 'Then the engineers picked it up and everything was reworked or re-engineered or remade. We're getting much quicker. With the early cars, we were waiting for re-engineered parts and that sort of thing.'

'It's quite a good process,' adds Waters. 'We've adapted as we've gone along simply so that we've got a more fluid process. I've come from the modern workshop and everything's completely different – if a part doesn't fit on a modern car, you just go and get another part! This is like going back in time. I've had to learn so much, and the guys have taught me no end of new skills and new methods.'

Although the specification of each car is worked out in advance, the small team is able to adapt certain elements of the car to its owner's wishes throughout the build process – be it the interior trim or even the colour of the grille mesh. Each customer even has the option to buy a tool kit, which is exactly the same tool kit that's used to build the continuation cars.

Once everything's completed, each car goes to Millbrook

Some things are best done the ■
old-fashioned way – marking up
the twin exhausts so that they
can be trimmed to length.

The trim is ordered in from Connelly, as it would have been in period, and is fitted at Newport Pagnell by Chris Brewer and the team.

for a 100-mile shakedown by Simons Hatfield and Dickinson, and any faults that show up are then rectified once it's back at Newport Pagnell. From receiving the bare chassis to leaving for Millbrook takes 4,500 man-hours, and both Alderman and Waters can testify to the fact that there has been a lot of overtime along the way.

'It's been a breath of fresh air to get this project,' concludes Alderman. 'We've had problems along the way but it's the best thing that's happened to us. I know a lot of Newport Pagnell people who used to work across the road who have retired and they love it: "How's the new car going?!" They can't believe it. Everyone had written Newport Pagnell off, really, and now we're back again.'

The last word should go to Spires, the man who dreamed up the whole adventure in the first place: 'To be fair, you couldn't have done what we've done 20 years ago. If you'd wanted to

make a DB4 G.T. continuation 20 years ago, you couldn't have done it to this level. You could probably have made two cars per years, but you couldn't have done it to this level, with this amount of accuracy and engineering integrity.

'If anyone said to me, "Would you do it again?", I probably would. But I'd certainly have to think twice about it! It's taken its toll on the team. Don't ever underestimate how difficult it's been. The car looks superb, it's the business, but it's been tough on everybody.

'I'm immensely proud of what we've be able to achieve in a very short space of time and there isn't a moment of the day when DB4 G.T. doesn't excite me. I go down to the workshop and it excites me. I sit in the car and it excites me. I walk around the Build Centre and the colours of the cars excite me. I'm very proud and passionate about it. If I wasn't, I'd be the wrong person to do this job.'

Chapter 8
PHOTO GALLERY

Given that Aston Martin has achieved so much success at Goodwood over the years, it's fitting that PP1 was photographed there by Max Earey before it went to its new owner in America. The marque claimed victory in all three of the Nine Hours races at the West Sussex venue – in 1952, '53 and '55 – plus Tourist Trophy honours in '59. And there's even been 21st-century success thanks to Simon Hadfield and Wolfgang Friedrich taking Project 212 to an unlikely victory in the 2013 Revival Meeting's RAC TT Celebration.

The DB4 G.T. remains one of the most beautiful of Aston Martins, and its versatile nature perfectly embodies an era in which such cars – whether built in Newport Pagnell, Maranello or Coventry – could be driven to the track, raced, and then driven home again. Restarting production more than 50 years after it came to an end proved to be even more of a challenge than the team at Aston Martin Works thought it would be, but the results are spectacular. And with all of the effort that went into this project, perhaps it's not surprising that the Touring-bodied DB4 G.T. will not be the last continuation car to emerge from the famous Tickford Street premises.

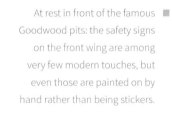

At rest in front of the famous Goodwood pits: the safety signs on the front wing are among very few modern touches, but even those are painted on by hand rather than being stickers.

DB4 Continuation – History in the making

■ The windscreen is the only glass panel – the side and rear windows are all Perspex. And whereas the DB4 used 16-gauge alloy for its outer panels, the G.T. went to 18-gauge in order to save weight. Note that all continuation cars have the larger style of bonnet scoop.

DB4 Continuation – History in the making

Left: rear flanks each feature a Monza-style quick-release fuel-filler cap. They feed the same 30-gallon aluminium fuel tank, which – when topped with the spare wheel – pretty much fills the entire boot.

A famous Aston Martin Lagonda numberplate above the equally evocative David Brown badge, which was remanufactured by the same company that made them in period. Note that '1 AML' has been hand-painted.

The G.T.'s distinctive cowled headlamps were later adopted on the DB4 Vantage and subsequently carried over to the DB5. As on PP1, the continuation cars feature neither front nor rear bumpers.

Right: sweeping through the Goodwood chicane. The intake for the oil cooler is pop-riveted in place – as was the original – and the technicians at Newport Pagnell hand-trim each grille to fit its individual aperture.

DB4 Continuation – History in the making

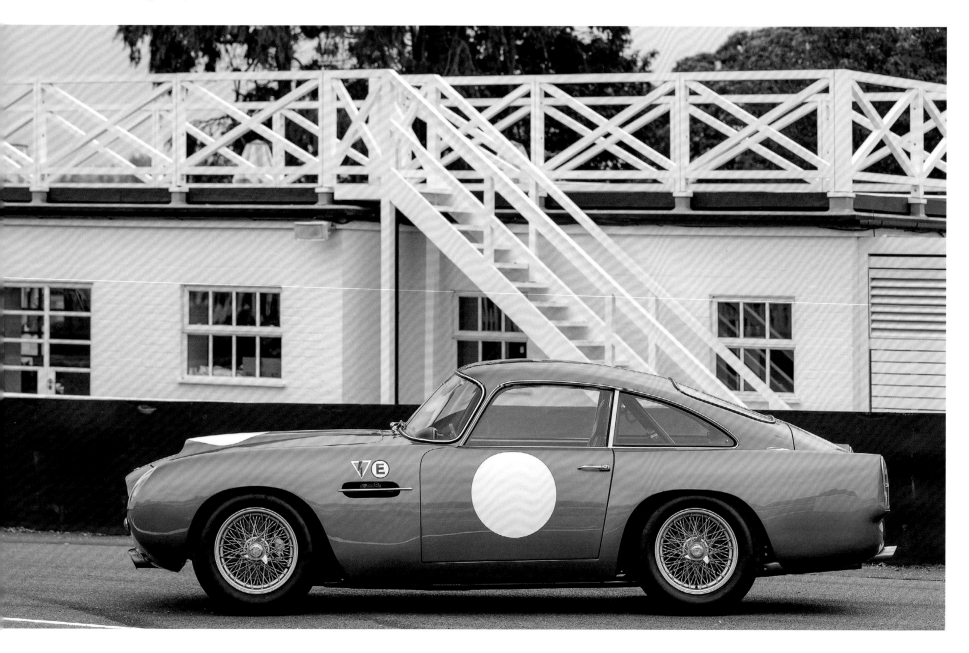

■ Being five inches shorter than the DB4 gives the G.T. a more aggressive stance. The length was saved from an area just ahead of the rear wheels, which made the G.T. a strict two-seater. All had frameless windows.

The attention to detail on the engine extends to the HT leads – they're finished in the correct yellow with a black stripe. Weber 45 DCOE carbs were standard on the G.T., but the Project racers were fitted with larger 50 DCOEs.

A DB4 G.T. in its natural habitat ■
– pressing on around a circuit.
The use of the original-spec
wheels, tyres and suspension
gives the continuation car a
suitably authentic feel.

Appendix 1
DB4 G.T. Build Data

DB4GT/0101/L   18.11.1959
Touring body; originally 001 – changed to 101 in February 1960

DB4GT/0102/R   31.12.1959
Touring body; originally 002 – changed to 102 in February 1960

DB4GT/0103/L   23.11.1959
Touring body; originally 003 – changed to 103 in February 1960; raced by Stirling Moss in Nassau

DB4GT/0104/L   20.03.1960
Touring body; originally 004 – changed to 104 in February 1960

DB4GT/0105/R   25.02.1960
Touring body

DB4GT/0106/L   06.02.1960
Touring body

DB4GT/0107/R   27.01.1960
Touring body

DB4GT/0108/L   04.03.1960
Touring body

DB4GT/0109/R   03.05.1960
Touring body

DB4GT/0110/R   21.06.1960
Touring body

DB4GT/0111/R   N/A
Touring body

DB4GT/0112/R   28.05.1960
Touring body

DB4GT/0113/R   19.07.1960
Touring body

DB4GT/0114/L   23.03.1960
Touring body

DB4GT/0115/R   27.06.1960
Touring body

DB4GT/0116/L   11.07.1960
Touring body

DB4GT/0117/R   17.07.1960
Touring body

DB4GT/0118/R   14.07.1960
Touring body

DB4GT/0119/L   15.03.1960
Touring body

DB4GT/0120/L   12.08.1960
Touring body

DB4GT/0121/R   16.07.1960
Touring body

DB4GT/0122/R   19.08.1960
Touring body

DB4GT/0123/R   08.11.1960
Touring body

DB4GT/0124/R   16.04.1960
Touring body; Lightweight specification; supplied to Tommy Sopwith of Equipe Endeavour; used by Ron Fry in 1961 registered LGL 400

DB4GT/0125/R   16.05.1960
Touring body; Lightweight specification; supplied to John Ogier of Essex Racing; registered 18 TVX

DB4GT/0126/R   23.09.1960
Touring body

DB4GT/0127/R   27.10.1960
Touring body

DB4GT/0128/L   14.01.1961
Touring body

DB4GT/0129/L   24.03.1960
Touring body

DB4GT/0130/L   12.12.1960
Touring body

DB4GT/0131/L   03.09.1960
Touring body

DB4GT/0132/L   15.04.1961
Touring body

DB4GT/0133/L   08.11.1960
Touring body; raced at Sebring in 1961

DB4GT/0134/L   13.10.1960
Touring body; raced in '61 by le Guezec (pictured right)

DB4GT/0135/L   29.09.1960
Touring body; raced at Sebring in 1961

DB4GT/0136/R   01.12.1960
Touring body

DB4GT/0137/R   21.12.1960
Touring body

DB4GT/0138/R   21.04.1961
Touring body

DB4GT/0139/R   18.03.1961
Touring body

DB4GT/0140/R   14.10.1960
Touring body

DB4GT/0141/L   02.01.1961
Touring body

DB4GT/0142/L   29.08.1961
Touring body

DB4GT/0143/L   23.02.1961
Touring body

DB4GT/0144/L   04.08.1961
Touring body; Kamm-style tail fitted in late 1960s;
rebodied as original in 1997

DB4GT/0145/R   22.04.1961
Touring body

DB4GT/0146/L   29.04.1961
Touring body

DB4GT/0147/R   26.01.1961
Touring body; raced by Jackie Stewart at
Charterhall in 1961

DB4GT/0148/R   17.05.1961
Touring body; rebodied at Newport Pagnell in 1967-'68
with DB5-style front and DB6 Kamm-style tail

DB4GT/0149/R   14.02.1961
Touring body

DB4GT/0150/R   03.01.1961
Touring body

DB4GT/0151/R   N/A
Touring body; Lightweight specification; supplied
to John Ogier; registered 17 TVX

DB4GT/0152/L   26.10.1962
Touring body

DB4GT/0153/L   29.11.1961
Touring body

DB4GT/0154/L   15.06.1961
Touring body

DB4GT/0155/R   05.06.1961
Touring body

DB4GT/0156/R   06.01.1961
Touring body

DB4GT/0157/R   01.03.1961
Touring body

DB4GT/0158/R   28.04.1961
Touring body

DB4GT/0159/R   23.06.1961
Touring body

DB4GT/0160/R   09.05.1961
Touring body

DB4GT/0161/R   08.06.1961
Touring body

DB4GT/0162/R   06.06.1961
Touring body

DB4GT/0163/R   25.05.1961
Touring body

DB4GT/0164/R   10.07.1961
Touring body

DB4GT/0165/R   15.05.1961
Touring body

DB4GT/0166/L   24.12.1961
Touring body; raced in 1961-'62 by Peter Lindner

DB4GT/0167/R   26.04.1961
Touring body; Lightweight specification; registered 40 MT;
Autosport road-test car

DB4GT/0168/L   14.03.1961
Touring body; Lightweight specification

DB4GT/0169/R   18.01.1961
Touring body; used in competition by Phil Scragg in 1961
registered 237 SPL

DB4GT/0170/R   05.09.1961
Touring body

DB4GT/0171/R   21.11.1961
Touring body

DB4GT/0172/L   23.08.1962
Touring body

DB4GT/0173/L   21.05.1962
Touring body

DB4GT/0174/R   05.09.1962
Touring body

DB4GT/0175/L   01.03.1963
Touring body; Lightweight specification

DB4GT/0176/R   26.10.1962
Zagato body

DB4GT/0177/R   06.12.1961
Zagato body

DB4GT/0178/L   08.03.1961
Zagato body

DB4GT/0179/L   04.02.1961
Zagato body; built at Zagato in Italy (pictured right)

DB4GT/0180/L   04.03.1961
Zagato body; built at Zagato in Italy

DB4GT/0181/L   01.03.1961
Zagato body; built at Zagato in Italy

DB4GT/0182/R   N/A
Zagato body; DP207 Lightweight specification; supplied to John Ogier; registered 1 VEV

DB4GT/0183/R   N/A
Zagato body; DP207 Lightweight specification; supplied to John Ogier; registered 2 VEV; rebuilt to DP209 specification following accident at Spa in 1962

DB4GT/0184/R   30.06.1962
Zagato body

DB4GT/0185/R   13.06.1962
Zagato body

DB4GT/0186/R   20.12.1961
Zagato body

DB4GT/0187/L   15.05.1961 (chassis only); warranty issued 10.08.1962
Zagato body; built at Zagato in Italy

DB4GT/0188/L   15.05.1961 (chassis only); delivered 17.06.1962
Zagato body; built at Zagato in Italy

DB4GT/0189/R   16.05.1963
Zagato body

DB4GT/0190/L   26.06.1962
Zagato body; bought by John Coombs and raced at Brands Hatch by Roy Salvadori

DB4GT/0191/R   N/A
Zagato body; DP207 Lightweight specification

DB4GT/0193/R   N/A
Zagato body; DP207 Lightweight specification

DB4GT/0194/R   N/A
Project 214 racer for 1963 season

DB4GT/0195/R   N/A
Project 214 racer for 1963 season

DB4GT/0199/L   20.12.1960
Zagato body

DB4GT/0200/R   10.03.1961
Zagato body; 1960 Earls Court Show car; raced by Stirling Moss for Rob Walker

DB4GT/0201/L   December 1960
Bertone-bodied Jet styled by Giorgetto Giugiaro; steel body; displayed at Geneva Salon in 1961

The continuation cars below are listed in the order in which they were built, rather than chassis-number order. The prototype was DB4GT/PP1/L …

DB4GT/0227/R   2017
Touring body; Lightweight specification

DB4GT/0219/L   2017
Touring body; Lightweight specification

DB4GT/0221/L   2017
Touring body; Lightweight specification

DB4GT/0212/L   2017
Touring body; Lightweight specification

DB4GT/0225/R   2017
Touring body; Lightweight specification

DB4GT/0206/L   2018
Touring body; Lightweight specification

DB4GT/0207/L   2018
Touring body; Lightweight specification

DB4GT/0213/R   2018
Touring body; Lightweight specification

DB4GT/0215/R   2018
Touring body; Lightweight specification

DB4GT/0203/R   2018
Touring body; Lightweight specification

DB4GT/0224/R   2018
Touring body; Lightweight specification

DB4GT/0218/L   2018
Touring body; Lightweight specification

DB4GT/0222/L   2018
Touring body; Lightweight specification

DB4GT/0217/L   2018
Touring body; Lightweight specification

DB4GT/0204/L   2018
Touring body; Lightweight specification

DB4GT/0208/L   2018
Touring body; Lightweight specification

DB4GT/0210/L   2018
Touring body; Lightweight specification

DB4GT/0211/R   2018
Touring body; Lightweight specification

DB4GT/0216/R   2018
Touring body; Lightweight specification

DB4GT/0209/L   2018
Touring body; Lightweight specification

DB4GT/0205/L   2018
Touring body; Lightweight specification

DB4GT/0223/L   2018
Touring body; Lightweight specification

DB4GT/0220/L   2018
Touring body; Lightweight specification

DB4GT/0214/R   2018
Touring body; Lightweight specification

DB4GT/0226/L   2018
Touring body; Lightweight specification

Note that 'R' and 'L' denote right- or left-hand drive

Sanction II Zagato-bodied chassis numbers
0192, 0196, 0197, 0198 (built January 1989 to July 1991)

Production figures
Touring body 100
Zagato body 19
Project 214 2
Bertone Jet 1
Sanction II Zagato 4

Note that two Sanction III Zagatos were built in 2000 using as their base standard DB4s – chassis DB4/0334/R and DB4/0424/R

Appendix 2
Specifications

DB4 G.T. ···

Built 1959-'63

Construction steel platform with Superleggera tubular steel frame, aluminium body panels

Engine all-alloy, twin-overhead-camshaft, 3,670cc inline-six, bore 92mm, stroke 92mm, three twin-choke Weber 45DCOE carburettors, twin plugs per cylinder, 9:1 compression ratio

Power 302bhp at 6,000rpm

Torque 270lb ft at 4,250rpm

Transmission all-synchromesh, close-ratio, four-speed manual, 9in twin-plate clutch, Salisbury 4HA hypoid bevel axle with Powr-Lok limited-slip differential, 3.54:1 final-drive ratio (optional 2.93, 3.31, 3.77 or 4.09)

Front suspension independent, via unequal-length double wishbones, coil springs and tubular dampers, anti-roll bar

Rear suspension live axle, coil springs, lever-arm dampers, trailing links, Watt linkage

Steering rack and pinion, 2.8 turns lock to lock

Brakes Girling discs all round, 12in front, 11in rear, twin master cylinders, no servo

Length 14ft 4in (4,354mm)

Width 5ft 6in (1,676mm)

Height 4ft 4in (1,321mm)

Wheelbase 7ft 9in (2,362mm)

Front track 4ft 6in (1,372mm)

Rear track 4ft 5.5in (1,359mm)

Wheels Borrani 16in 72-spoke wires

Tyres 6.00 x 16

Weight 2,735lb (1,240kg)

Continuation DB4 G.T. ·································

As DB4 G.T. apart from…

Built 2017-'18

Engine 4,211cc (bore 98.5in, stroke 92mm), 9.81:1 compression ratio

Power 350bhp at 6,000rpm

Torque 350lb ft at 5,000rpm

Transmission four-speed, straight-cut, close-ratio 'box with dog engagement

Weight 2,670lb (1,220kg)

Zagato ···

As DB4 G.T. apart from…

Compression ratio 9.7:1

Power 314bhp at 6,000rpm

Final drive 3.31:1

Length 14ft (4,267mm)

Width 5ft 5.25in (1657mm)

Weight 2,634lb (1,195kg)

Performance figures of 0167, as tested by Autosport in 1961

Top speed 152.5mph

Standing quarter-mile 14 seconds

0-30mph 2.4 seconds

0-50mph 4.6 seconds

0-60mph 6.4 seconds

0-80mph 10.2 seconds

0-100mph 14.2 seconds

Maximum in-gear speeds of DB4 G.T. with standard 3.54:1 axle ratio

First 54mph

Second 78mph

Third 108mph

Top 22.6mph per 1000rpm

DB4 G.T. exterior colours ·························

Almond Green

Black Pearl

Bristol Red

California Sage

Caribbean Pearl

Deep Carriage Green

Desert White

Dubonnet

Elusive Blue

Fiesta

French Racing Blue

Goodwood Green

Ming Blue

Pacific Blue

Pale Primrose

Peony

Sea Green

Shell Grey

Snow Shadow Grey

Carmine

Indigo

Wedgewood Blue

White

White Magnolia

Acknowledgements

First and foremost, thanks must go to everyone at Aston Martin who helped during the writing of this book. Simon Bench went above and beyond in his efforts to co-ordinate everything from interviews to photography, and both Paul Spires and Simon Hatfield were generous with their time.

The enthusiasm for the continuation project ran throughout Newport Pagnell and, on each occasion that I visited, the engineers and technicians were endlessly patient as I went around pointing at things, asking what they were and how they worked. Thanks, in particular, to Dave Alderman and Joe Waters for taking time out of their hectic schedules in order to chat.

Donna Bannister, curator of the Aston Martin Heritage Trust, and John Wood were a huge help in terms of sourcing archive images and letting me rummage through the Trust's library and many archive documents. In terms of the modern photography, thanks to Max Earey and Noel Read.

And last but by no means least, thanks to Philip Porter, Leanne Banks, Luke Robinson and the rest of the team at Porter Press for entrusting me with this book. It's been a fascinating project.

Bibliography

AM Quarterly
Autosport magazine
Aston Martin – A Racing History, Anthony Pritchard
Aston Martin – The Post-War Competition Cars, Anthony Pritchard
Aston Martin DB4GT, Stephen Archer and Richard A Candee
Aston Martin DB4/5/6 – The Complete Story, Jonathan Wood
Classic & Sports Car magazine
Factory-Original Aston Martin DB4/5/6, James Taylor
Motor Sport magazine
Racing with the David Brown Aston Martins, John Wyer
Stirling Moss Scrapbook 1956-'60, Stirling Moss and Philip Porter

Index